100**ROCK**GROOVES FOR**ELECTRIC**BASS

Learn 100 Bass Guitar Riffs & Grooves in the Style of the Rock Legends

DAN**HAWKINS**

FUNDAMENTAL**CHANGES**

100 Rock Grooves for Electric Bass

Learn 100 Bass Guitar Riffs & Grooves in the Style of the Rock Legends

ISBN: 978-1-78933-386-2

Published by **www.fundamental-changes.com**

www.fundamental-changes.com

Over 12,000 fans on Facebook: **FundamentalChangesInGuitar**

Instagram: **FundamentalChanges**

For over 350 Free Guitar Lessons with Videos Check Out

www.fundamental-changes.com

Cover Image Copyright: Shutterstock, Roman Voloshyn

Contents

Introduction

There's no style of bass playing more immediate, more powerful, or downright satisfying to play than rock.

The harmonies, techniques and rhythms can be simple, or they can be incredibly intricate. For us bass players, rock is an endlessly interesting genre that remains as popular as ever.

In this book we will explore the style, techniques and tones of some of the greatest rock bassists of all time. In the process, I will show you some of the main constituents of rock basslines so that you can a) create your own riffs, lines and fills, and b) hear music with a more educated ear.

When you strengthen your ear, figuring out basslines becomes much easier and you become a more rounded musician as a result. Immersion is always a key part of mastering any musical style, so I encourage you to listen to as many styles of rock music as you can. Find the players and bands you like, then figure out as many of their basslines as you can.

This book will help you in that quest, as I'm about to teach you everything you need to know to become a great rock bass player.

Let's get started.

Dan

Get the Spotify playlist to accompany this book now by scanning the QR code below:

Get the Audio

The audio files for this book are available to download for free from **www.fundamental-changes.com.** The link is in the top right-hand corner. Simply select this book title from the drop-down menu and follow the instructions to get the audio.

We recommend that you download the files directly to your computer, not to your tablet, and extract them there before adding them to your media library. You can then put them on your tablet, iPod or burn them to CD. On the download page there is a help PDF and we also provide technical support via the contact form.

www.fundamental-changes.com

Over 12,000 fans on Facebook: **FundamentalChangesInGuitar**

Instagram: **FundamentalChanges**

For over 350 Free Guitar Lessons with Videos Check Out

www.fundamental-changes.com

Chapter 1: Early Beginnings

The advent of Motown in the 1960s produced one of the all-time greats of bass in James Jamerson. John Entwistle is to rock bass what Jamerson is to Motown. It's astonishing that someone so technically proficient and forward thinking came to prominence in rock music's epoch. Entwistle was a player who didn't need any influences because he became *the influence* for countless rock bassists and remains one of its benchmarks to this day.

Entwistle wrote the book on tone and technique. Snarly, high gain, bright, overdriven bass tones combined with revolutionary new techniques to complete his sound (more on those techniques later). He was a dextrous player, despite his nickname "The Ox" (actually derived from his ability to drink copious amounts of alcohol), who used fingerstyle, plectrum, tapping, harmonics, and various plucking techniques including "the typewriter" (striking the strings right over the fretboard with the first, second and third fingertips to create an aggressive metallic sound).

Entwistle is also responsible for the first bass solo heard on a rock record. *My Generation* showcases his outrageous, confident approach and it still sounds fresh and exciting today.

Another huge influence in the bass world, Jack Bruce was a more accomplished and formally trained musician. He studied jazz bass early on and won a scholarship to the Royal Scottish Academy of Music and Drama. His melodic, fluid style emerged as a direct result of his musical influences. In the band Cream, his blues and jazz background helped form a new sound that would influence players like Geddy Lee and Geezer Butler.

For many bass players, Entwistle, Bruce and Chris Squire make up the holy trinity of rock bass influences. Another Englishman, Squire was a founding member of the progressive rock group Yes. His tone was instantly recognisable, with a clear, direct, aggressive attack, produced with a plectrum (a Herco, recently reissued by Dunlop). The way he held the pick contributed to his tone, allowing only a tiny bit of the plectrum tip to protrude from his fingers, causing part of his thumb to strike the strings.

The huge innovation in his bass sound came from his Rickenbacker bass's Rick-O-Sound feature – a stereo output that enabled him to feed a bass amp via the warm neck pickup, while sending a lead-type tone to a guitar amp. The resulting blend was pure lead bass! You can learn more about achieving this kind of tone in the Rock Bass Gear chapter at the end of the book.

Gear checklist: Entwistle experimented a lot with his basses and used everything from Alembic to Status. Later in his career, he favoured a signature Warwick Buzzard (loosely based on his hybrid Fender-neck/Gibson Thunderbird body basses). Much of his early work with The Who saw him using a Fender Jazz with stock flatwound strings (used on *My Generation*) although he also used Precisions. His amp set up was an elaborate affair with various effects and overdrives in a rackmount unit with huge cabinets. Earlier on, he used Hiwatt amps.

Jack Bruce used a short scale Gibson EB3 bass for much of his early work, although a lot of *Fresh Cream* was recorded with a Fender VI, tuned EADGBE, like an electric guitar but an octave lower. Later, he used a fretless Warwick Thumb bass. The EB3 has a deep, low end grit to it that sounds different to the Fenders most people were used to hearing at the time. The tone came down to the 30.5" scale length plus the large neck humbucker (there is also a mini-humbucker at the bridge). For amplification, he used a stack of Marshall 4x12 cabinets with 100-watt heads.

Think Rickenbacker 4001 and you immediately conjure images of Chris Squire rocking out on stage. His split signal tone produced strong bass fundamentals with rich overtones. He used Herco plectrums and Ampeg and Sunn amps.

Recommended Listening:

My Generation – The Who

Who Are You – The Who

Won't Get Fooled Again – The Who

I Feel Free – Cream

Sunshine of Your Love – Cream

Badge – Cream

The Fish (Schindleria Praematurus) – Yes

Roundabout – Yes

Siberian Khatru – Yes

John Entwistle

Our first example features one of rock music's most important devices: the *riff*. A riff is simply a repeating pattern and rock music is littered with them.

Entwistle probably would have played this first example as written (using no open strings), but feel free to try it with them. Pluck right in the middle, between the end of the fretboard and the bridge, to achieve a good rock tone. Also strike the strings from a greater height, down towards the frets. This produces a metallic tone as the string strikes more of the fret. Rock tone is often about aggression and intent, so focus on your sound as you go through the book.

Example 1a

A riff can be delightfully simple. Add some articulation and a confident repeating rhythm and, hey presto, instant rock. The next example uses a rock staple, the *minor pentatonic* scale, shown below organised into a useful pattern

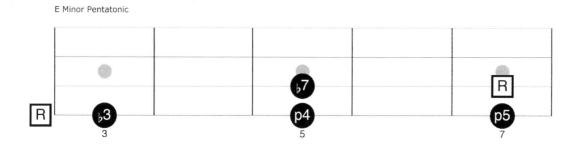

You can combine the previous riff with this next one as they both use E Minor.

Make sure to completely cut off the open E string after the third 1/16th note in this phrase by gently flattening your fretting hand fingers against the string. Look out for the quick hand shift during the last eight notes of the riff, where you need to quickly jump your first finger from fret 3 to 5.

Once you have this riff under your fingers, use the diagram above to create a similar one. Pay attention to the fret numbers below the diagram – the first note is on the 3rd fret not the 1st!

Example 1b

The next three examples all work together and there is a backing track for them that you can practice along to. The lines are in the style of the iconic *My Generation* bass solo. In keeping with that feel, the 1/8th notes are swung and there are triplets for the fast runs.

The tempo is fast (160bpm) and even the 1/8th notes fly by quickly, so slow things down if you need to and don't use the backing track until you can play up to tempo.

The first part uses the E Minor Pentatonic shape from the previous example. For the bend in bar six, use your second and third fingers together to squeeze the string down towards the floor. Immediately release to fret 7 when you've finished.

Example 1c

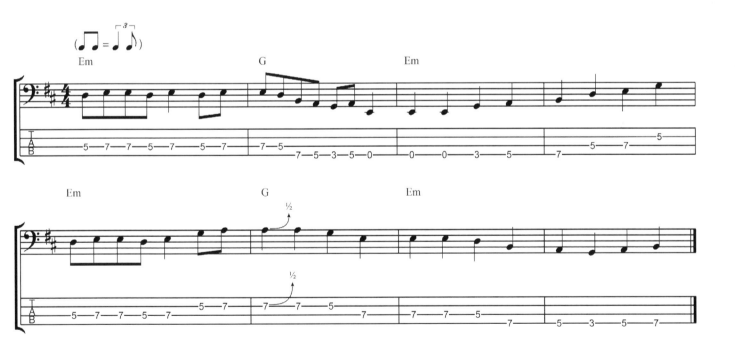

Example 1d shifts to the upper register using a very common minor pentatonic pattern. Learn this shape inside out.

E Minor Pentatonic

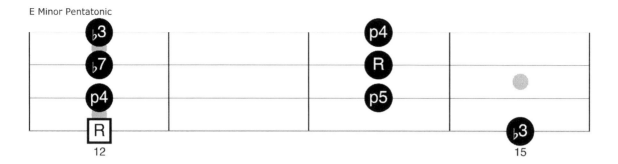

Listen to the audio example to catch the 1/8th note triplet rhythms. They're fast, so isolate them and alternate between your first and second fingers to play them.

Example 1d

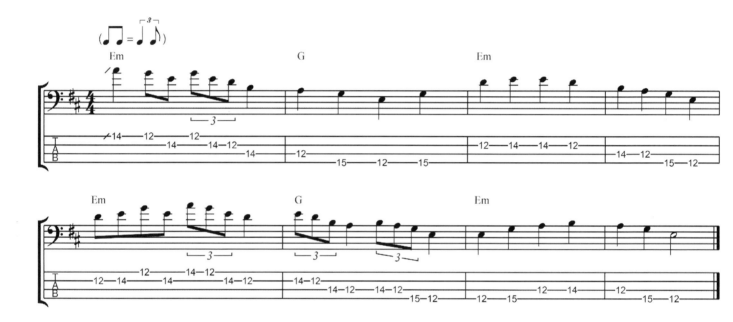

The last section of the solo uses notes on one string and has some typical Entwistle-like plucking hand finger combinations. You may be used to plucking just with the first and second fingers, but Entwistle included the third finger to aid faster playing.

Use traditional first and second finger plucking if you need to but do try the plucking pattern indicated below and incorporate the third (you'll need to move your fingers fast!)

Slide into the E on the 12th fret and slide down to the G on fret 3 all the way from fret 10. The latter is a *shift slide* where you pluck the note that you're sliding into. There's also a *legato slide* at the end of bar six, where you *don't* pluck the note when you slide into it.

Articulations like this add attitude and flair to rock basslines. Take your time strengthening and coordinating your fingers so that you can instantly call on these expressive techniques. Refer to my book *Creative Technique Bass Exercises* for more on this topic.

Example 1e

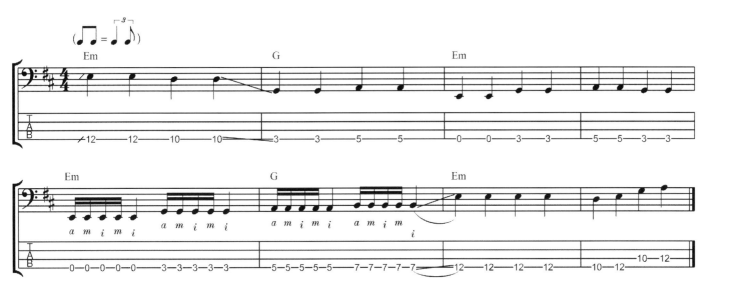

Jack Bruce

We've already seen how important the minor pentatonic scale is to rock music. Add one note to this pattern and we get the minor blues scale. You can hear this in action in *Sunshine of Your Love*. Here's the shape, which is used in the next example.

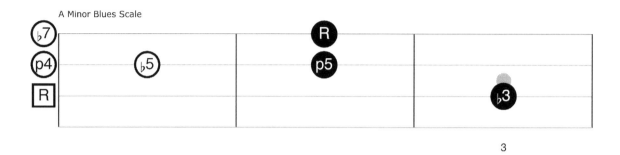

The added note is the b5 interval. When used as a passing note, it produces a bluesy sound that is used a lot in rock riffs.

Example 1f

Bruce's first love was jazz, and he was a big fan of using the b7 interval in a pattern also used by blues and funk bass players.

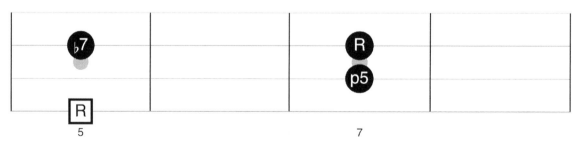

The next example uses notes from the above pattern to move between A7 and G7 chords. Use the same fingering in each bar, shifting quickly to the root note with your first finger. When stretching from a root note to a 5th or octave, it's often much easier to fret with your fourth finger instead of your third. This lessens the stretch and keeps the wrist straight, avoiding any prospect of injury while playing relentless lines like this.

Example 1g

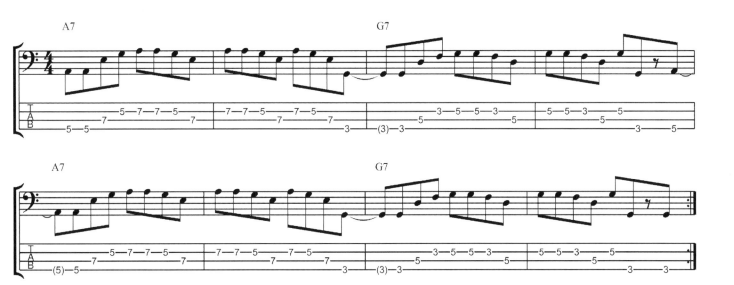

Rock emerged from Blues, RnB and Soul, and much of Cream's early work was centred around the 12-bar blues form. This extremely common chord progression uses just three chords (Em, Am and Bm in the minor blues example that follows).

This example in E Minor has a simple driving rhythm to tie the line together. One thing rock music teaches us is that simple is often best. Notice the use of chromatic notes (notes from outside the scale) to connect the chords – a jazz trick Bruce liked to use in his basslines.

There's an E Minor Pentatonic fill in the last bar that sets things up nicely for the repeat. Use the backing track to practice some of these ideas for yourself. The following shape will help with fills and note selection.

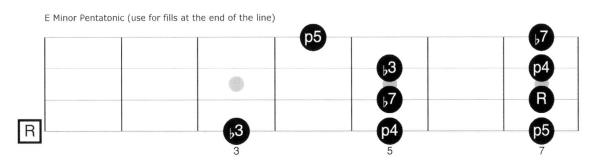

E Minor Pentatonic (use for fills at the end of the line)

Example 1h

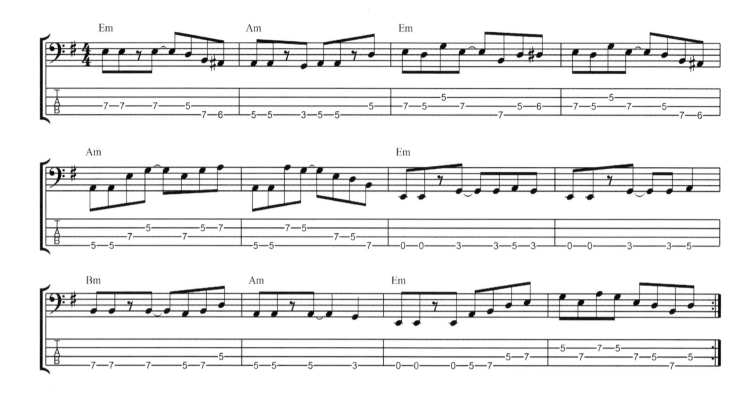

The next example returns to the blues scale for an up-tempo, straight-ahead rock riff. Aim to play this one at around 130bpm eventually, but practice it slowly at first. Pay attention in particular to the slide into the Bb note on fret 6. Execute that slide with your fourth finger, so that the third is in position to fret the next note. Shift to fret 7 while you're plucking the open E string.

Example 1i

Example 1j uses notes from the key of D Minor to create a melodic bassline. Use the shape below along with the chord symbols above the bars to come up with your own line. There's a backing track for you to experiment over.

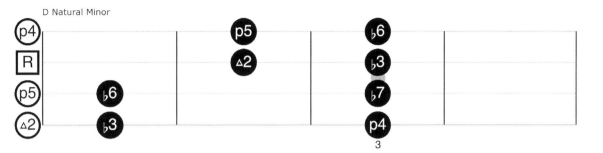

When coming up with your own version, stick to a simple rhythm and follow the root notes of the chords. Use scale notes from the diagram to travel smoothly from one chord to the next and you'll be sounding like Jack Bruce in no time.

Example 1j

Chris Squire

Chris Squire was exclusively a plectrum player, so the following examples are all notated with pick markings, but feel free to use your fingers if you prefer.

Roundabout is one of the most famous picked rock riffs and is almost funk-like in its use of articulation and rhythm. Example 1k is an intricate riff containing hammer-ons and ghost notes played with a plectrum. The best way to approach it is to take it beat by beat and follow the markings closely.

If playing with a plectrum (give it a go, with practice you'll get used to it!) use a constant down-up motion. For the hammer-ons from the open D string, use your first finger. This will keep you locked into the groove and make it easier to match the downstrokes and upstrokes to the correct notes.

Aim to play the line at around 125bpm in time, but slow things down to half speed to get the riff under your fingers.

Here are some quick tips for playing with a plectrum:

- Hold it between your thumb and first finger, so that not much of the tip protrudes from your fingers. This gives you more control

- Anchor the heel of your palm somewhere on the body around the E string. You can even rest on the E string itself if you're not playing it

- Optionally, resting your fourth finger on the body under the G string can also help you to maintain a consistent hand position

Example 1k

The next example is a bassline that includes some lead-bass style melody. Squire loved his basslines to be prominent and often played high register fills.

At the end of bar two, shift to the C note on fret 10 to play it with your second finger. You're then in position to play the remaining notes. In the last bar, you only have a 1/16th rest to shift! Play the C on fret 8 with your first finger, then get your fourth stretching, ready to play the 12th fret G string.

The pull-offs might take a bit of work but they're great for strengthening the fretting hand fingers.

Use the backing track for this one (80bpm).

Example 11

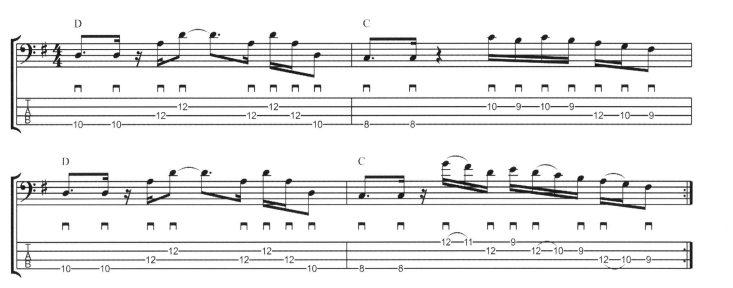

Squire was a master of improvisation and, in live situations, often soloed like a guitarist. If you YouTube any live version of *The Fish* you can hear him in action.

The next three examples explore his style and technique in an improvised bass solo. The harmony used comes from the E Dorian scale (the second mode of the key of D Major). Practice playing the shape below over the backing track to get this sound into your head. The Dorian sound is used *a lot* in rock music.

Here's a three-note-per-string pattern for E Dorian with the root note on the E string. Three-note-per-string patterns are really useful for legato techniques (hammer-ons, pull-offs and slides).

E Dorian Three Note Per String Pattern

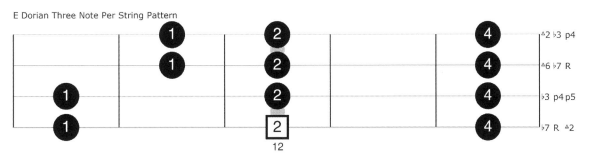

The next three examples fit together, so learn each one and then combine them.

Follow the TAB closely for the next example and compare the notes to the above diagram. Once you realise that basslines adhere to certain patterns, memorising them becomes much easier, as does improvising.

Example 1m

Here we have some technical fireworks with some fast alternate picking in conjunction with hammer-ons. If using your fingers, make sure you use alternate plucking. Follow the fingering pattern and slow this one right down making sure your hammered-on notes are as loud as the picked (or plucked) ones.

Explore this technique with some of the other notes from the diagram above.

Example 1n

Squire often played ideas based on moving notes along one string. Here's the E Dorian scale arranged along the D string.

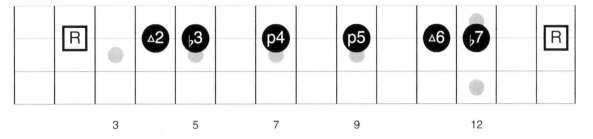

This example will test your slides and hand shifts. Use your second or third finger to fret the notes when you slide. First pick (or pluck) then slide to the next note, making sure to maintain fretting pressure. Then shift as you go, using the third and first fingers for the notes at the end of the second bar.

There are many possible fingering patterns here, so do experiment. Use your first finger for the slides starting at the end of bar four. Take some time with this, there's a fair bit of coordination required for this pick slide technique. Build it up slowly and make sure you get the timing bang on.

Example 1o

Chapter 2: Classic Rock

Classic Rock is one of the most popular subgenres of rock, even though the term is a fairly loose description. Bands from this genre were generally commercially successful and enjoyed massive radio play and huge stadium-filled tours.

Many of these bands played accessible, memorable riffs – the backbone of much rock music. Riffs are so satisfying to play and write, and in this chapter you'll learn how.

Few bands were as iconic as AC/DC. Cliff Williams joined the band in 1977 and his tasteful playing has been heard on every album since, including their breakaway success *Back in Black*.

Only a handful of musicians are instantly recognisable by a one-word name, but Lemmy is one such icon. Born, Ian Fraser Kilmister, he founded Motörhead and went on to embody the hard-living rock stereotype. His playing and tone were equally as ferocious, with a huge stack of amps providing a heavily overdriven bass tone. His sound was more akin to that of a rhythm guitarist and his use of power chords was something not many bass players were doing at that time. This contributed to a huge sound which inspired Heavy Metal bands such as Metallica.

On the radio-friendly pop side, Journey are one of the best-selling bands of all time, with over 80 million record sales. Bassist Ross Valory played on many of the big hits, including *Don't Stop Believin'*. His style is a perfect blend of driving groove and melodic creativity, often mirroring what the guitars and keys are playing. He's an underrated and extremely tasteful player and someone you should definitely check out.

Gear checklist: Cliff Williams is a long time MusicMan StingRay bass and D'Addario strings user. The punchy humbucker pickup and active circuitry make the StingRay a popular choice for rock bass players (it's also great for funk). He uses an Ampeg SVT-4PRO with an 8x10 cabinet.

Lemmy is synonymous with the Rickenbacker 4001. Like Chris Squire, he used one exclusively throughout his career. He nicknamed his amp "Murder One" – it was a 1976 Marshall Super Bass Head that he used with 4x12 and 4x15 cabinets.

Ross Valory uses MusicMan StingRay basses these days but he played the unusual Ovation Magnum bass in Journey's heyday (he also used the equally strange looking Steinberger L2). He was a pioneer of tuning a 4-string bass to B E A D, to get the range of a 5-string with the optimum playability of a 4-string. Ampeg was the choice of most rock bass players in those days and Valory was another user.

Recommended Listening:

Back in Black – AC/DC

For Those About to Rock (We Salute You) – AC/DC

Come and Get It – AC/DC

Ace of Spades – Motörhead

The World is Yours – Motörhead

Stay Clean – Motörhead

Escape (Greatest Hits Live version) – Journey

Don't Stop Believin' – Journey

To Play Some Music – Journey

Cliff Williams

The first two Cliff Williams-style riffs are real headbangers. They both use the minor blues scale, common to classic rock. Here's the pattern the riffs are derived from. Learn it, pick a really simple rhythm leaving plenty of space and make your own riffs up from it.

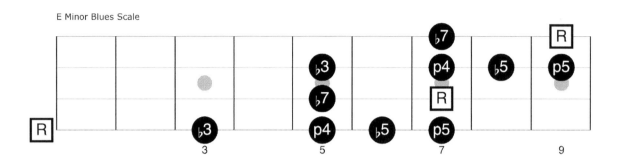

E Minor Blues Scale

Example 2a uses the first four notes of the scale and includes plenty of rests. Look how simple it is to create a rock riff! However, you must play with complete control and excellent timing if it is to sound authentic. Set your metronome to 90bpm and play this riff as precisely as you can. Keep the open E string notes short in length.

Example 2a

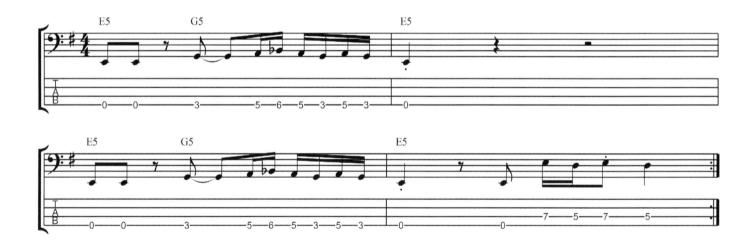

You can play this riff along with the previous one, as it's the same key and tempo. Follow the TAB, shifting up the neck quickly after playing the open E string. Control the note length of that E by gently patting your fretting hand fingers down against the strings to mute the note.

To play the run at the end of bar two, shift position while playing the first open E.

Example 2b

One of the most common rhythms you'll encounter in rock bass playing is the 1/8th note. They look and sound simple to play but they're really not. You can instantly tell an accomplished bass player from a novice by the way they play 1/8ths. The next line will help you to work on them.

Keep the note lengths short and don't deviate in terms of speed, tone production or volume. Consistency is the aim of the game! To this end, set your metronome to 120bpm (although you can try different tempos) and lock into the groove.

Listen to the audio example first. In the first two bars, the 1/8th notes are to be played short and in the final two bars, slightly longer. This manipulation of note length is something you should master and is a technique you can use to differentiate sections of a song. For fretted notes, you can control the note length purely using your plucking fingers.

Example 2c

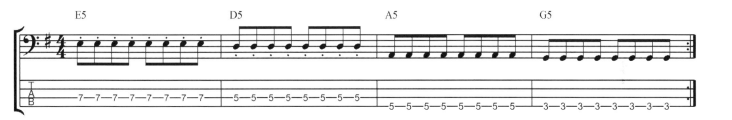

Let's take a closer look at note length with another 120bpm groove using the E Minor Blues scale. Play the first two E notes for their full 1/4 note duration, then keep things legato (smooth and connected with no gaps between the rhythms) before playing the last four notes very short.

Example 2d

For Those About to Rock (We Salute You) – especially the live versions – contains a fast section with 1/8th notes and tasty minor pentatonic fills. This is an effective device to use in your playing, especially when you insert fills at the ends of phrases (usually every two to four bars).

In the next example, there is a simple 1/8th note bass line followed by minor pentatonic fills every other bar. Use the backing track and the shape below to create some fills of your own.

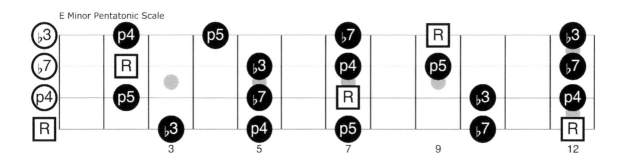

Example 2e is played quite fast (140bpm), so if that's too much for now, set a metronome to a more manageable tempo and work up to full speed. If you increase the tempo by 5bpm every few practice sessions, you'll develop speed and stamina in no time.

Play the notes in bar three with your first finger, so you're ready for the upper register fill in the next bar. The penultimate bar is the trickiest, as you need to watch out for the slide. Slide up to fret 14 with your third finger and you'll be in the right position to play the remaining notes of the fill.

Example 2e

Lemmy

Don't worry, you don't need a Murder One size rig to sound like Lemmy! However, a heavily distorted bass sound is integral to the tone, so use a distortion, overdrive or fuzz pedal with the gain set accordingly.

Lemmy also used a plectrum, but as with the Chris Squire style lines, use your fingers if you're not up to speed with a plectrum.

Here's a relatively simple line that uses mostly downstrokes. Keep the same downstroke motion going when you get to the 1/16th notes, adding in the upstrokes. This is *alternate picking*. Aim to play all the Lemmy riffs at around 130bpm, starting slowly then building up speed.

Example 2f

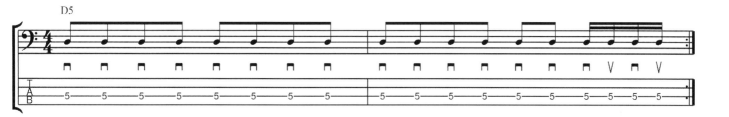

Alternate picking followed by a hammer-on, then more alternate picking, is an excellent way to build fast, fluid lines. Here's the same line as the previous example, with the addition of a C note that is picked then hammered onto the D. Pick the C with a downstroke then hammer-on with your third or fourth finger. Aim for the hammered note to be as loud as the picked one. It might take some time to build up the technique, as it requires a fair bit of strength.

Once you have it at a slow speed, incorporate the other notes and play along with a metronome. You can combine the previous example with this one.

Example 2g

A similar idea using tied notes creates a signature Lemmy move most famously heard on *Ace of Spades*. There are a lot of upstrokes involved in this line and they all occur on an upbeat. Go through the line slowly and follow the pick markings. Notice that your picking hand is set in one steady, constant motion.

Remember to anchor your picking hand either with your fourth finger, the heel of your palm, or both.

There's no need to lift up your first finger, so keep it on the 3rd fret. If you hammer-on with your fourth finger, you can use the longer second and third fingers to mute the E string while your first finger backs onto the G.

You definitely need to work on muting, especially when playing a heavily overdriven bass. An unmuted, uncontrolled heavy bass tone sounds awful!

Example 2h

Power chords were something Lemmy used a lot. They are notated with an accompanying "5" (as in the D5 of the previous example) to indicate their formation. A power chord consists of a root note and a 5th interval. When distortion is added, it sounds like pure rock 'n roll.

Here's the classic power chord shape. Play both notes together at the same time.

In this example, play the D note on fret 5 with your third finger, so that you are already fretting the power chord with fingers one and four. This way, your fingers don't have to move too much and you can focus on strumming the D and G strings together with one downstroke.

Example 2i

This line is exactly the same, but you need to shift up two frets to a G power chord. Use the same fingers for the F5 and shift your hand while your fingers remain set in the power chord shape.

Example 2j

Ross Valory

The following five examples can all be played together as they use the same key and tempo.

Although in the key of G Major, the first two lines here use the D Major Pentatonic scale to outline the D major chord (see diagram below).

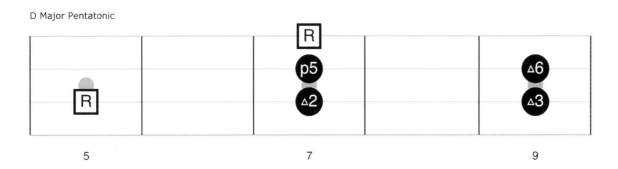

D Major Pentatonic

Keep the 1/8ths in the first and third bars short and consistent. Play the notes in the first bar with your first finger, then slide into fret 9 from two frets below. The fill ascends this much-used major pentatonic pattern – a fantastic scale to use over any major chord.

Coming out of the fill, you can play the D open, which gives you time to shift your hand back down to the C on fret 3. Aim to get this up to around 140bpm. Use the backing track for this example and the next.

Example 2k

Valory is a master of the melodic bass line, much like one of the all-time greats, Pino Palladino. In the next example, after the pentatonic fill, return to the D this time playing it at fret 5.

The fill is quite involved, so I suggest following the fingering patterns, which are a little unconventional but get the job done. If you find another way you like, go for it.

Slide up to fret 12 using your third finger then fret the next two notes with the same finger. Next, pull off to the 11th fret. I find it easier to use my second finger for that note. Follow the fingering closely from then on, paying particular attention to the slide from fret 10 to 9 using the first finger.

Example 2l

One of the great things about rock bass is that it can be technically challenging, so you never get bored and you can really stretch out and express yourself.

However, the one-note riff also reveals the beauty of the genre. Simplicity is just as effective as all the impressive fast notes. Listen to *Separate Ways (Worlds Apart)* for a brilliant example.

The next line takes inspiration from that song, using only an E note and some syncopation (playing notes off the beats) to create tension and excitement. Play along to the backing track and lock onto the guitar riff.

Use your fretting hand fingers to mute the E string to keep the notes quite short.

Example 2m

You can play the next example coming out of the last one, as it's like going into a chorus section from a main riff.

Again, the line is simple, using mostly 1/4 notes with some melodic connecting notes. The key to this line is the intent with which you attack and play the notes. It's the bassist who drives the band (along with the drummer!)

Play the 1/4 notes bang on the beats, plucking with a slightly harder touch to make it sound more aggressive. Pay attention to the dots by the notes. They indicate a *staccato,* which means to play the note short and detached. Listen to the audio example for clarification.

Example 2n

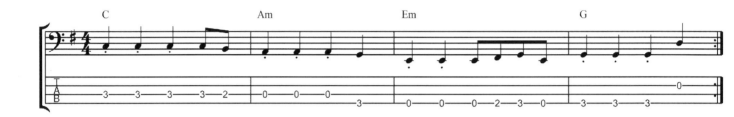

Journey are one of the greatest rock power ballad groups of all time, with *Don't Stop Believin'* being one of their most famous songs. The next example is in a similar style in the key of G Major.

The chord progression is I V vi IV (G, D, Em, C) and the diagram below highlights where the root notes of those chords lie. Those notes appear in more than one place, but restrict yourself to the ones shown here. It looks a little complicated at first!

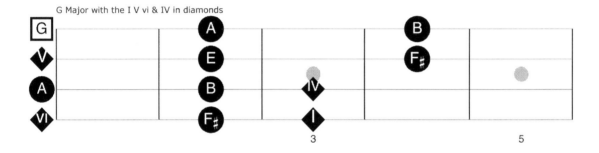

I want you to be able to create your own memorable riffs and rock lines and here's a good opportunity. Play the I V vi and IV in that order, then use some of the surrounding scale notes to connect the root notes in a pleasing way. You will come up with loads of cool lines. Make sure to write down or record your best ones so you don't forget them.

Play through this example, which was written exactly as described above. Associating basslines with scale patterns and creating new ones in this way will really help improve your ear and composition skills.

Example 2o

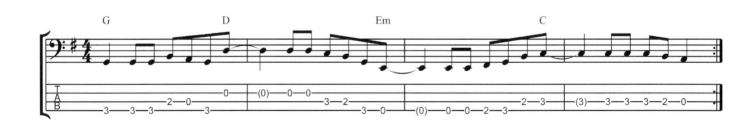

Chapter 3: Heavy Metal

Heavy Metal is characterised by heavily distorted guitars, aggression and power. It's one of the most popular genres of rock music and originated both in the UK and USA.

Three of the most prominent bands were Led Zeppelin, Deep Purple and Black Sabbath, all of them formed in 1968.

Born to musical parents, John Paul Jones became a prominent session bass player in London. He played on hundreds of sessions for Decca Records from 1964 up to the formation of Led Zeppelin. These included songs with Jeff Beck, Dusty Springfield and Rod Stewart, as well as a whole host of other artists. You can hear many influences in his playing including James Jamerson and jazz players such as Charlie Mingus.

His musical versatility, dextrous technique, and composition skills were a huge asset to Zeppelin. Along with drummer John Bonham, they formed a rhythm section steeped in Motown, Soul, Blues, Jazz and Funk. This gave them an unmistakable feel that contributed greatly to their mass appeal.

Black Sabbath had a sound more closely associated with traditional Heavy Metal. They detuned their guitars, played tight chunky riffs, and sang about songs with dark and horror-infused themes.

Geezer Butler was a founding member of the band and a key component of their massive sound. He sometimes tuned his bass down to C# F# B E (you can hear this on the *Master of Reality* album). His style with Sabbath was supportive and he often doubled the guitar to create signature rock riffs. A former guitarist himself, he had a melodic sensibility that was often expressed in between riffs.

You could describe Metallica's original bass player as the Jaco Pastorius of metal bass. Cliff Burton left the world far too young at 24, after a road accident, but the legacy he left remains. He helped shaped the sound and style of the band perhaps most synonymous with the term Heavy Metal.

Burton's virtuosic touch, blistering technique, and ferocious tone combined to create many memorable moments, perhaps best encapsulated by the beginning of *Anesthesia*. He played with a range of bass tones from clean to heavily distorted, used mainly first and second fingerstyle plucks, and applied plenty of technical facility.

Gear checklist: John Paul Jones mainly used a 1962 Fender Jazz bass bought for around $250 (a bass like that is now worth closer to $10,000!) You can get the sound with any modern bass that has two single coil pickups. When his Fender began to give up on him, he endorsed high-end boutique Alembic basses. For amplification he used Acoustic 360 amp heads coupled with the 361 cabinet. Unlike many rock bassists of the day, Jones tended to play clean, adjusting his technique or swapping instruments to achieve different tones.

Currently, Geezer Butler plays his own signature Lakland 4-string and Ashdown amp. The first few Sabbath albums were recorded using a late '60s Fender Precision. Later, he used a Dan Armstrong Plexiglass after his Precision was damaged. He was then closely associated with Birmingham-based luthier John Birch, who created a number of Gibson EB-inspired custom basses for him. He recorded *Black Sabbath* with a Laney amp and a Park cabinet.

Cliff Burton liked to use very light strings (35-90) which helped him achieve his virtuosic, guitar-like moments. He used just one bass, the Rickenbacker 4001. Later on, he added a Seymour Duncan single coil guitar pickup at the bridge to help him to get the lead guitar tone (coupled with distortion) that he so often used. He also had a Gibson mud bucker pickup installed in the neck position, and modified the stock bridge pickup.

When that bass started failing him (there's a theme here of rock bassists' instruments suffering under the heavy toll of rock 'n roll!) he used an Aria Pro II SB1000. He used a variety of amps including a Randall bass head with a 1x18 cabinet. He also used Sunn amps and Road cabinets.

Recommended Listening:

Black Dog – Led Zeppelin

Immigrant Song – Led Zeppelin

Kashmir – Led Zeppelin

Paranoid – Black Sabbath

War Pigs – Black Sabbath

After Forever – Black Sabbath

Anesthesia – Metallica

Master of Puppets – Metallica

Orion – Metallica

John Paul Jones

The John Paul Jones/John Bonham rhythm section had a groove that made people dance and nod their heads. In contrast to the later high-tempo, frantic heavy metal riffs that emerged, they liked to play slower. This first example is played at 80bpm.

Use the open A string in bar one to shift up to the high A on the 7th fret. Then use the next open A to shift back down.

Example 3a

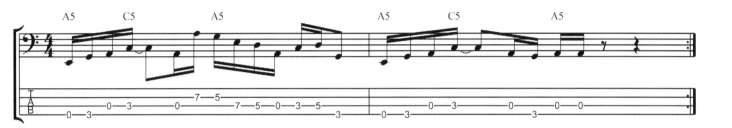

You can combine the next riff with the previous one and there's a backing track for this example. Listen to the guitar riff on the backing track. The bassline weaves around the 1/16th note riff and doubles with the guitar. It's mostly root notes, 5ths and octaves with some melody from the A Natural Minor scale. Here's the shape, so you can practice your own lines over the backing track.

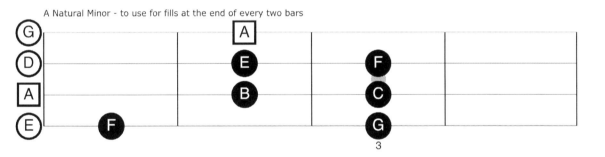

Slightly busier fills work over the F chord because it's at the end of a two-bar phrase. Aim to play your fills there.

Example 3b

The next example is fast and frenetic with a double time drumbeat (120bpm). There's a backing track with just drums so you can hear what a double time drumbeat sounds like – you'll recognise it when you hear it. There's something exciting and primal about playing these types of lines!

Make sure you can play the hammer-ons with full control at the faster tempo. If it's tough, slow things down and make sure the hammer-on and the two plucks that follow are tight and in time, with the hammered note nice and loud.

Watch for the shift right at the end. Once you get to the last note, slide back down to the beginning. The slide sounds great but also gets you back into position.

Example 3c

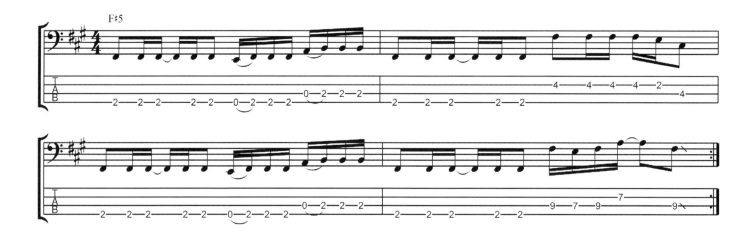

Led Zeppelin created some of the most memorable rock riffs, including *Black Dog* and *Immigrant Song*. The next two examples are riffs in the key of F# Minor and use the minor blues scale. This is a good rock key as you can use the open E string to get heavy.

Experiment with your own riffs in a similar style using this shape. Try that at 85bpm (the same tempo as the audio example for this and the next example).

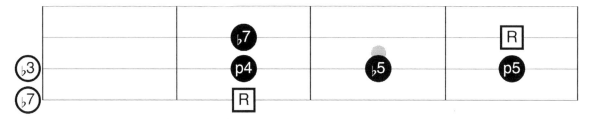

F# Minor Blues Scale - use this shape to create riffs

Example 3d

You can play the next example all in one position. Use your third or fourth finger to fret the C# on the 4th fret, D string. The hardest part of this riff is the end section, which require lots of fast alternate plucking moving from fretted notes to the open A string. A high level of coordination is required for that section, so practice it slowly and keep all the notes short and precise.

Example 3e

Geezer Butler

Our first Geezer Butler-style line is a fairly simple 1/8th note riff with some hits at the end. It should be played at around 150bpm, so the 1/8ths are actually quite fast. Watch out for the jump from the G note to the open D string. If you want to play that D at fret 5 of the A string, feel free to do so.

Example 3f

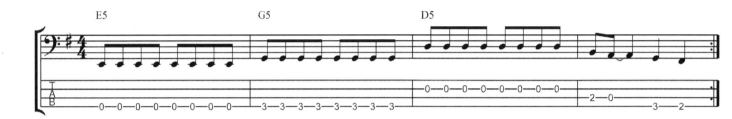

One of the requirements for a rock bass player is to be able to play an interesting bassline over one chord. Geezer Butler was fond of using the minor pentatonic scale to improvise melodic lines and fills over guitar solos or song sections.

This example uses E Minor Pentatonic. Here are the shapes across the neck, which you can use with the backing track to make up your own ideas in the style of this example.

Don't underestimate how useful this scale can be (and not just in rock bass playing). The E Minor Pentatonic scale contains only the notes E, G, A, B and D. However, as you can hear from the audio example, there's so much you can do with this collection of notes.

Take your time to learn the patterns below, then start creating music with them. That's the best way to learn any scale.

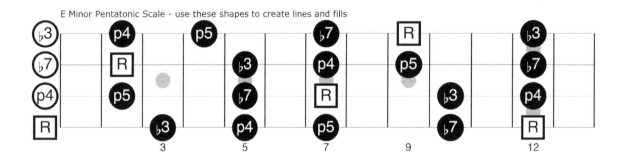

The trick is to come up with one simple idea and rhythm from which you break out, using the notes of the scale in different registers. Start by playing a shape or two up, then down, but with an interesting rhythm. Even that will sound amazing.

Listen to the audio example for inspiration and study the line.

Example 3g

Look at the last example one more time. It is pure fingerstyle with zero articulation. Articulations are the expressive techniques that bring bass playing to life. Let's now play exactly the same line with some hammer-ons, pull-offs, slides and vibrato.

Notice how much more *rock* the line sounds!

You need to play some of the open notes fretted to facilitate these techniques, so follow the TAB closely. If you find one technique particularly challenging, write that down to work on in future practice sessions.

My book *Complete Fingerstyle Bass Technique* has a whole section on these articulations with exercises to help master them.

Example 3h

Many bass players tend to like the sound of fretted notes rather than open ones, as they sound more even and you get a more consistent tone. It's also much easier to control note length. In this example, make sure you mute the E string immediately after the second E.

Example 3i

Add two notes to the minor pentatonic and you get a natural minor scale. This is another dark sounding set of notes that's used a lot in rock music. Here it is in one octave, low down on the bass, where you can make up all kinds of rock riffs.

E Natural Minor

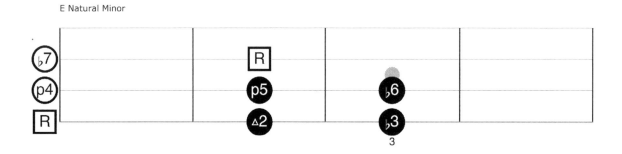

The next line uses this scale and is in 12/8 time. To count this, count as you would in 4/4, but subdivide each beat into three 1/8th notes i.e. **123 123 123 123** = one bar.

Listen to the audio example to hear how it should go and remember to keep your foot tapping on the beats.

Example 3j

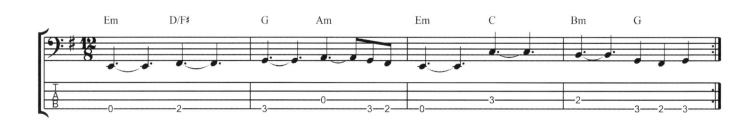

Cliff Burton

The first Cliff Burton-style example requires some fast plucking finger speed. At this tempo (135bpm) 1/16th notes fly by quickly, so make sure you strictly alternate between first and second fingers. Burton used his fingers to play very fast passages, so this proves you don't necessarily need a plectrum for extreme speed!

Example 3k

Metal riffs do tend to be fast and furious. Here's another one that you can combine with the previous example. The rhythms are syncopated, so refer to the audio example if you need to. Keep the notes short and make sure to mute the E at the end of each bar.

Example 3l

Fast tempos, low register notes and syncopation are some of the features that make up metal riffs. Another popular device is the triplet. Almost nothing else sounds as heavy as these three 1/8th notes stuffed into the space a 1/4 note normally occupies. If you're unsure of the rhythm, listen to the audio example for the next line.

There's a slide and some hammer-ons in this line. After the G note on fret 3, shift quickly to fret 12 before sliding back down the neck.

Example 3m

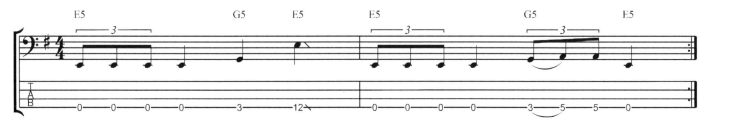

In the intro to *Anesthesia*, Burton shows off his creative side, using all manner of articulations and rhythms in a classical-inspired bass solo. The next two examples can be played together. To get the sound, tweak a distortion or fuzz pedal to a high gain setting and use a wah pedal if you have one.

The first bar outlines an E minor triad and the second bar is an *inversion*. An inversion is a chord or triad where the lowest note is the 3rd, 5th or 7th, rather than the root. In bar two, the D/F# chord (usually pronounced "D over F#") is a D major triad with the 3rd (F#) as the lowest note. This gives the line a classical flavour many metal artists love.

There are many plucking patterns you can use, so I advise you to experiment. Burton would often pluck notes on adjacent strings both with his first finger, before following with his second finger. This technique makes it easier to traverse strings quickly.

Example 3n

Legato means smooth in Italian and refers to the use of hammer-ons, pull-offs and slides to create fast, fluid lines. Burton would embellish his lines using these techniques.

The best way to play the next example is to isolate the legato sections and work on your coordination until you feel somewhat comfortable. Play it slowly every day then introduce a metronome clicking on all beats. Set it slow at first then build up to 130bpm.

Follow the TAB closely. In bar two, after the hammer-on, keep plucking with alternate fingers and focus on nailing the timing of the four 1/16th notes.

In the last bar, pluck only once, then execute the hammer-on followed by two pull-offs. Follow the fingering pattern and keep your first finger fretted at all times, as that's the note you pull off to. This requires a bit of a stretch in the fretting hand, so if you feel any pain, stop immediately and rest. Build your ability to stretch over time, as well as working on your hammer-on and pull-off technique. You need dextrous fingers to play some rock bass lines but never play through the pain barrier. Instead, build up your technique by small increments each week.

Example 3o

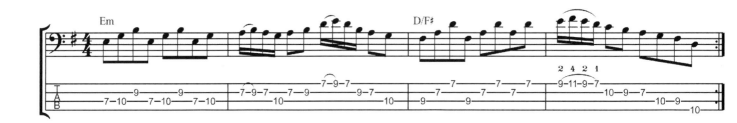

Chapter 4: Progressive Rock

Progressive rock took some of the virtuosity of the metal genre then ramped things up. Progressive rock musicians are the true virtuosos of the rock world, which is one reason why it's such an acquired taste amongst music fans.

Modern progressive rock is characterised by long instrumental sections, odd time signatures, exotic modes and technical wizardry. It's no surprise that many people can't (or won't) listen to it. It's often cruelly described as "where music meets maths" and branded a style that only musos love. Some of that may be true, but it's also true that progressive rock has given the musical world some of its greatest moments. It's a rich tapestry where there are no creative boundaries and musicians can flex their chops as they please.

Rush went through various iterations before settling on their power trio formation in 1974. Their bass player, Geddy Lee, is one of the single most influential rock bass players of all time. Les Claypool, John Myung and Steve Harris all cite him as a major influence. Ever the perfectionist, it was in fact Claypool who inspired Lee to add more funk into his playing. As a result, his style is characterised by a complete freedom to go where he likes.

Listen to *Leave That Thing Alone* (the 2011 live in Cleveland version is great) and you can hear Lee's full, rich bass tone with a layer of overdrive on top of his high-end Jazz bass rasp. That rock tone, allied with his ferocious technique and funk sensibilities, make for thrilling listening.

John Myung plays for perhaps the most famous modern prog rock band, Dream Theater. He plays a 6-string bass and has a unique three-fingered plucking technique that allows him to double very fast guitar and keyboard lines. His extended range bass enables him to play below E to really add weight, while giving him high register access for harmonics and chords. It also means he doesn't have to shift his fretting hand as much as on a 4- or 5-string.

Justin Chancellor of Tool plays the bass in a unique way, and his use of chords, articulation and effects contributes greatly to the band's success. A lot of Tool's music is recorded in Drop D (the E string is tuned down to D) which adds more beef while opening up unusual playing opportunities. *The Pot* is a good example of a riff based around an open low D.

Gear checklist: Geddy Lee is famous for his different eras of gear. He owns a huge collection of basses (check out *Geddy Lee's Big Beautiful Book of Bass*) but it was the Rickenbacker 4001 and, later, the Fender Jazz bass, that he made his mark with. He started with a Precision bass though, so has used pretty much everything (including Steinberger and Wal basses). His main bass now is his black 1972 Fender Jazz.

He has a signature Tech21 pedal that is well worth checking out. It allows you to layer a distorted bass tone over a strong, clean tone that retains its low end. That arrangement gives rise to a monstrous bass tone that is especially useful to thicken the bottom end in a trio setting. However, it sounds brilliant in any rock context.

John Myung plays a signature MusicMan Bongo 6-string. Don't let the looks and name put you off, this is a seriously powerful bass powered by an 18volt preamp. He plays Ashdown amps and uses rack-mounted processors and effects including a Fractal Audio Axe-Fx.

Justin Chancellor is another player who likes to experiment with different basses and a plethora of effects. His main recording and touring bass is a Wal 4-string that he likes for its mid-range and ease of playability. He uses (cheap) Boss delay and flanger pedals, as well as various overdrives. A constant in his recording chain is a Demeter VTBP-201S preamp. For amps, he favours two Gallien-Krueger 2001RB heads and Mesa Boogie 4x12 and 8x10 cabinets.

Recommended Listening:

Leave That Thing Alone – Rush

YYZ – Rush

Tom Sawyer – Rush

The Dance of Eternity – Dream Theater

Metropolis—Part I: "The Miracle and the Sleeper" – Dream Theater

Caught in A Web – Dream Theater

Schism – Tool

The Pot – Tool

Forty Six & 2 – Tool

Geddy Lee

Example 4a involves lots of hammer-ons, which require good coordination between the hands. Hammer-on from the B to C note in bar one with your first and second fingers, and prepare your first finger to pluck the low E immediately after the E on fret 2 of the D string.

Use the open E to quickly shift your first finger to the F on the 1st fret. You can then shift back into position when you play the open A string.

You could also play the entire line in first position, avoiding any shifts, if you prefer. There are many ways to play the same line on a bass guitar, so do experiment to find what is most comfortable for you.

Example 4a

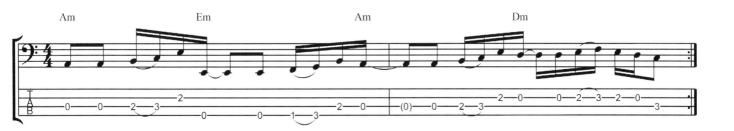

The next example can be combined with the previous one. Isolate the hammer-on and pull-off at the end of bar one and play through it slowly. The key to playing fast phrases like these is to nail the timing between the articulations and the plucking. This can only be mastered at slower tempos.

Use the open A string at the beginning of bars two and four to shift your hand into position for the subsequent melodic phrase.

Example 4b

The classic Rush riff on *YYZ* is in 5/4, known as an *odd time signature*. They are odd in number but also in nature, as these meters are not as easy to tap your foot to. They are, however, staples of progressive rock and really fun once you can count them.

5/4 means that there are five (top number) 1/4 note (bottom number) beats in every bar. The trick is to split the bar into sections that are easier and more familiar to count. You could, for instance, count 5/4 as a three and a two. Once you have the riff under your fingers though, it's often easier just to focus on that familiar unit and *feel* the rhythm more than strictly counting all the beats.

Give it a try with the next example. Play though one bar at a time, tapping your foot on the beat and counting to five. Once that feels comfortable, play both bars. You should reach the point where the pattern under your fingers guides you as much as your counting. This one should be played at 170bpm.

Example 4c

7/4 is another common prog time signature, which has seven 1/4 note beats per bar. The riff in *Tom Sawyer* is a great example. With this time signature, splitting it into a four and a three makes it feel much easier to play. Let's take the notes from the previous example and turn them into 7/4.

To begin with, take the first six notes and just play those. That's essentially 4/4 and should feel easy. Then work on the remaining notes – the last three beats of the bar. Once it feels comfortable, combine all the notes while tapping your foot on the beats.

Beat one comes around earlier than you expect if you're not used to playing in seven. But like anything, it becomes "normal" with practice! Listen to the audio example to get the feel and phrasing in your head.

Example 4d

The next example uses the open A string to bounce around to different positions on the neck. Play this riff at 110bpm and follow the TAB closely. Use the open A to quickly shift your fingers into position before returning to the repeating riff around frets 5 and 7.

Example 4e

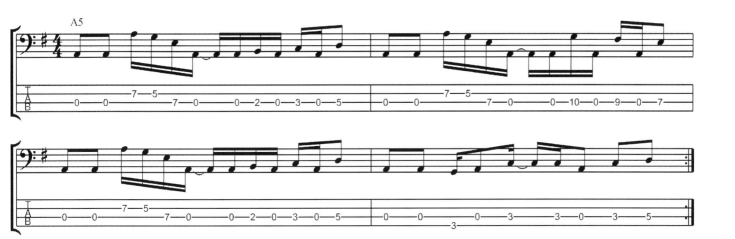

John Myung

Dream Theater are the one prog rock band who throw the proverbial kitchen sink at their writing. Odd time signatures, exotic scales and blistering unison runs all feature.

The next example uses the Phrygian mode (the third mode of the major scale). The minor second interval between the first two notes imparts a wonderfully dark flavour. Here it is illustrated in one octave. Notice that it is exactly the same as a natural minor scale with the exception of the b2 (comparing a scale to one you know well can make it easier to memorise).

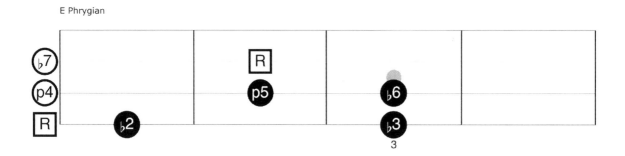

At the end of this first riff, you will need to shift your hand up to the E on the 7th fret. Use the preceding notes on the open E to make the jump, then shift back down while playing the next batch of open Es.

The fast run at the end is executed with hammer-ons. Pluck the E then hammer down onto the F, then the G, with fingers two and four.

Example 4f

Writing odd time signature riffs can yield some rhythmically complex, unique patterns that are perfect for prog. In Example 4g there are two bars of 5/16 followed by a bar of 7/16. The 5/16 time signature is five 1/16th notes per bar, and 7/16 is seven 1/16th notes per bar. However, don't be intimidated by this! Take each bar on its own, slow things right down and count in the following way:

For the 5/16 bars, split your counting into a two and a three.

Count, "one, two, one, two, three" twice for the two bars of 5/16.

Next, count "one, two, three, four, one, two, three" for the bar of 7/16.

This makes it easier to count and feel the subdivisions.

This is easier *heard* than *read*, so listen to the audio example to get the phrasing. Before long, and with plenty of practice, it will begin to feel normal, so do persevere!

Example 4g

A feature of many Dream Theater lines is a classic metal riff followed by an intricate unison run at the end of the phrase. The next example follows that formula with a head-banging riff followed by a run using the exotically named Phrygian Dominant mode.

This is a very metal sounding scale that's worth knowing if you want to create evil sounding riffs (it's actually also used a lot in flamenco music). Compare the following diagram to the one in Example 4f. It differs from the Phrygian mode by one note, having a major third. It's amazing how much difference one note can make to the colour and mood of a scale. Make up some riffs using this pattern:

E Phrygian Dominant

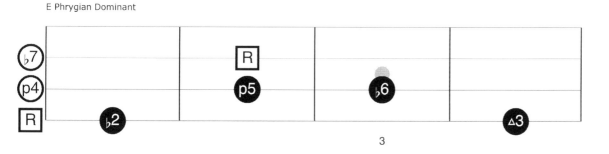

In the next example, follow the one-finger-per-fret fingering pattern in the last bar. You'll need to be ready to shift up one fret from the previous position.

Example 4h

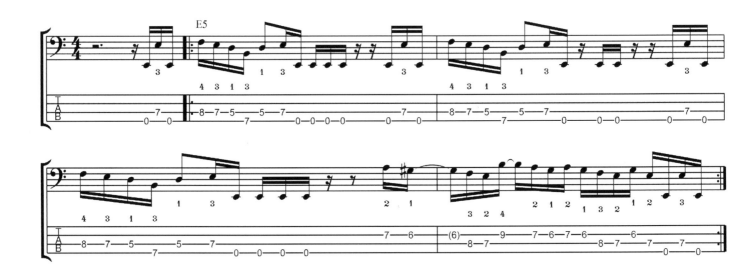

You can play the next riff in conjunction with the previous one. Watch out for the 1/32nd notes in bar two. At the tempo of 90bpm they're not too difficult to play, but refer to the audio example if you need to. There's a backing track for this one which combines this riff (with the drums playing a double-time feel) with the riff in the previous example.

Example 4i

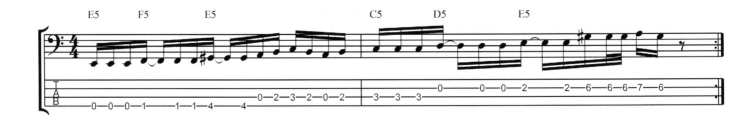

Another Dream Theater feature is to mix classic sounding 4/4 riffs with an odd time signature. This acts to displace the rhythms and adds tension and surprise to the music. This is a fast tempo 160bpm riff with a drum beat backing track, so you can practice the transition from 4/4 to 5/4 and back again.

Example 4j

Justin Chancellor

Justin Chancellor has stated how much he loves 7/4 and the first example in his style uses that time signature. Tap your foot and count to seven (at a fast tempo, around 170bpm), getting used to beat one arriving slightly earlier than you might be used to. Make sure to keep the note lengths short on the open D notes, using your fretting hand to mute.

Example 4k

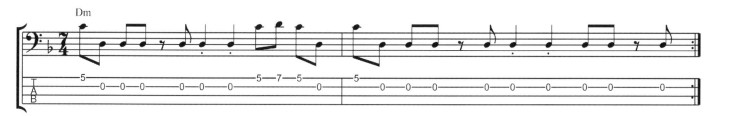

The next three riffs can be played together. Example 4l uses the open D string as a pedal note while playing a melodic line on the G string. As you are playing the open D string, shift your hand up and down the neck, making the hammer-ons and pull-offs as loud as the picked notes. Chancellor almost exclusively uses a plectrum but play with your fingers if you prefer. These lines will sound amazing with a little bit of distortion.

Example 4l

Another Chancellor favourite is Drop D tuning. There are many really interesting ideas to explore using this tuning that open up a completely different world to standard tuning. Tune your E string down a whole step to a low D. That low D is responsible for a serious amount of heavy rock basslines!

Try the pick suggestions in the next example but use your own approach if you find something more comfortable. Play all the notes in first position, apart from the notes in the last two beats of bar two. Shift your first finger to the 3rd fret while you're picking the low Ds.

Example 4m

Tool play plenty of heavy riffs and one innovative use of the drop D string is an unusual but highly effective power chord. Chancellor plays the low D and the standard open D along with two fretted Ds an octave apart. The result is a fat, resonant, jangly chord that sounds amazing.

To play it, strum from the lowest to the highest strings and control the muting with your picking hand. Use the palm of that hand to touch all the strings, muting them enough to enable you to control the length of the chord, which should be strummed with downstrokes throughout. You'll need that muting technique for the last chord of the bar.

Example 4n

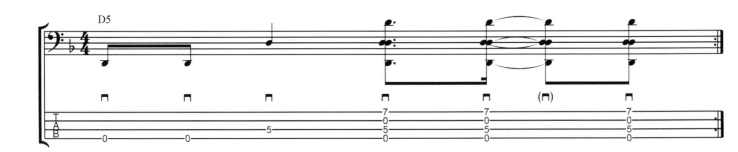

Tune your bass back to standard tuning. This example is a picked chordal riff in A Minor that allows the open A and E strings to ring out. It's in 6/4 and should be played at 150bpm.

First, you'll need to split the line up to get it all together. Take it one bar at a time and listen to the audio example. Use your thumb, first and second fingers to pluck the strings as an alternative technique to using a plectrum.

Make sure to let the notes ring out and use one-finger-per-fret-technique, playing right on your fingertips. This will stop parts of your fingers accidentally choking a string. Remember, we want the notes to ring out for this line.

Chords like this can be awkward to play if you've never tried them before, so go easy, especially if you feel any pain in the fretting hand thumb or wrist joints.

Example 4o

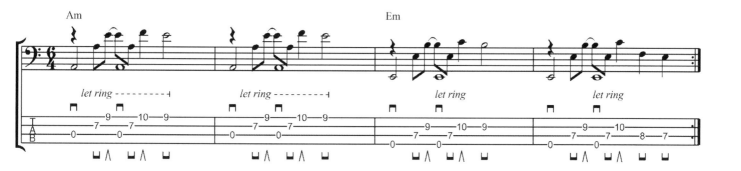

Chapter 5: Funk Rock

Almost any style of music can and has been fused with rock to create a subgenre. Some of these styles are popular and some just didn't work. The bass players featured in this chapter are hugely influential musicians from massive bands. Hip hop, funk, metal and rap styles permeate their music, but the attitude and aggression of rock is never far away.

Apart from the accolade of being one of the top ten richest bass players in the world, Flea may be one of the most influential. His fiery brand of slap and fingerstyle funk, with a bright, beefy tone has catapulted him into bass god status.

Red Hot Chili Peppers influences range from punk and funk to alternative rock and rap. Flea's partnership with Chad Smith helped to cement the band's characteristic sound. His groove laden, melodic, rhythmic basslines are a huge part of the band's style, with many songs built around a bass riff.

Funk and rock have many similarities including their basic units of music. Rock players call them riffs, while funk players call them grooves but, either way, both genres use repeating hooks to grab the listener. Flea has melded both styles with flair and flamboyance, and these hooks are always front and centre of the music, live and in the studio.

Doug Wimbish is a session player of great repute and was part of the house band for Sugarhill Records. He didn't play on their biggest hit, *Rappers Delight,* but he was high profile enough to be top of the list to replace Bill Wyman when he left the Rolling Stones. Wimbish eventually lost that gig to Darryl Jones but went on to play for everyone from Annie Lennox and Carly Simon to Michael Bolton, and on Mick Jagger's solo work.

However, the band Living Colour was the vehicle for his signature style. His use of effects was ground breaking and something not many bassists were embracing at that time. Effects like the Digitech Whammy and massive sub bass effects placed his bass playing in the foreground.

Les Claypool influenced one of the greatest rock bassists, Geddy Lee. To have that kind of reach you have to be a heavyweight and Claypool is one of the most unique voices on bass guitar. With his Carl Thompson 6-string fretless and unusual techniques, he stands out from the crowd. He uses strumming, slapping, chordal fingerstyle, tapping, and all manner of articulations to create weird and wonderful basslines.

While his band Primus emerged from the alternative rock and metal scenes of the early '90s, much of his playing is rooted in funk. If you listen to *Silly Putty*, his slapping and use of power chords is reminiscent of Stanley Clarke. He cites Clarke as an influence, as well as Bootsy Collins, Larry Graham and bass players from a wide spectrum of genres.

Gear checklist: Flea has a signature Fender Jazz based on a pre-CBS stacked knob '60s model. During the height of his technical powers in the 90s, he played MusicMan StingRay basses, although much of *Blood Sugar Sex Magik* was recorded using a Wal bass. He plays Gallien-Krueger amps live. One of his most famous sounds is the distorted intro on *Around the World*. That was produced using a Boss ODB-3 Bass Overdrive.

Doug Wimbish has played Spector basses for years, most notably the NS-2. It would be easier to list the effects pedals he *hasn't* used! Nothing is off the table and I suggest you YouTube his bass rig and select the tones you like. The Digitech Whammy is integral to his sound (check out *Nothingness* for a brilliant example, where he uses it with a sliding harmonic on a fretless bass). He loves using sub bass effects live like the Dod Meatbox. This is a pedal to use sparingly and make sure your speakers can handle it!

Les Claypool is a long-time user of the boutique and highly unusual looking Carl Thomson basses. He has various models including a 6-string fretless that he slaps and taps on. He has an overdriven tone nearly all the time (even when slapping) that comes from his Ampeg or Mesa Boogie amps and uses various effects from the likes of Line 6 and Fractal Audio.

Recommended Listening:

Sir Psycho Sexy – Red Hot Chili Peppers

Aeroplane – Red Hot Chili Peppers

Around the World – Red Hot Chili Peppers

Silly Putty – Primus

Tommy The Cat – Primus

Hamburger Train – Primus

Love Rears Its Ugly Head – Living Colour

Wall – Living Colour

Song Without Sin – Living Colour

Flea

Funk basslines are characterised by syncopated rhythms and repeating patterns. Note length is especially important and needs to be controlled via a combination of fretting hand muting and plucking hand placement.

For our first Flea-style example, it's crucial to tap your feet on all the beats, so you can place the rhythms more securely.

For example, the first note of bar two is the second 1/16th note and that can be hard to feel.

Subdivide the beats into 1/16ths and count **1** e & a, **2** e & a, **3** e & a, **4** e & a

If you prefer a more percussive counting style you can express this as,

da-ga-da-ga, **da**-ga-da-ga, **da**-ga-da-ga, **da**-ga-da-ga

If you get used to subdividing the beats like this and count religiously, your sense of rhythm and timing will improve no end.

Make sure to give the last note some real vibrato to funk things up. Bend the string rapidly up and down.

Example 5a

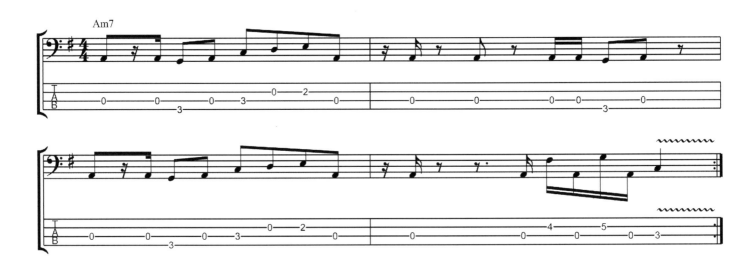

The extra funky vibe of the previous example came, in part, from the syncopated rhythm but also the notes used. The Dorian mode is the second mode of the major scale and is built for funk. Let's take a closer look at it. Here is a one octave A Dorian scale. Notice how the notes are exactly the same as A Natural Minor with the exception of the sixth note, which is raised a half step.

This one note makes all the difference!

A Dorian

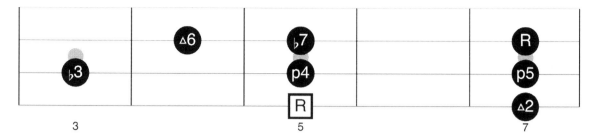

Example 5b uses the above pattern, except the A is played open. Since it's in the same key as the previous example, you can combine them.

Another great tip when it comes to minor keys is to use the minor pentatonic scale for fills or to embellish lines. Try it at the end of the riff using this pentatonic shape. There's a backing track for you to practice with.

A Minor Pentatonic

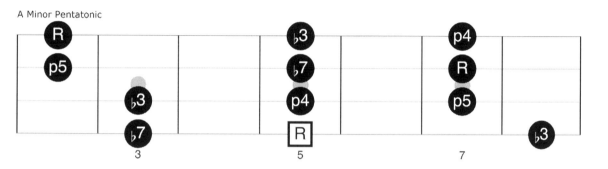

Ghost notes are an excellent device to use in funk rock bass playing and this next line features them. Ghost notes are muted notes that emulate the ghosting technique drummers use to create grooves.

To play clean ghost notes in this example, mute the A string with your fretting hand fingers while your first finger hovers over the 3rd fret, ready to play the C.

During the next set of ghost notes, shift your first finger up two frets ready for the hammer-ons.

Use the pentatonic shape above to make up your own fills to go with this riff and experiment over the backing track.

Example 5b

You really need to dig in and summon your best punk spirit for the next line. The notes are simple, the rhythms are syncopated, but it's the energy you bring to a line like this that makes or breaks it. Listen to *The Greeting Song* to get the vibe we're going for.

The pentatonic shape from the previous example will work with this line if you want to add in some fills.

Example 5c

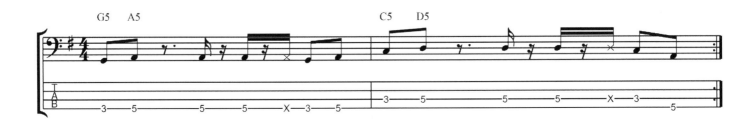

Not all Flea's playing is flashy and in your face. This example is in the style of one of his more supportive basslines (*Dani California* is a good example). It's based on octaves, which you can play using either your third or fourth finger. I find using the fourth lessens the hand stretch and straightens the wrist out a little, which is great for technique and avoiding strain.

Whichever way you play them, keep your hand set in the octave shape, so you can easily shift it to the root note you need.

Keeping the first of the 1/8th notes short and the second long creates a bouncy groove that works well for this line.

Example 5d

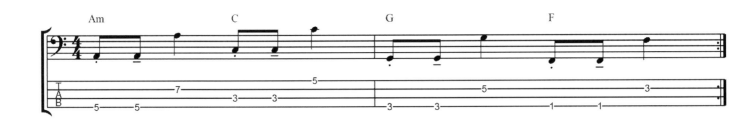

Let's look at the same line with more funk added. More often than not, this mean adding in more syncopation and articulations like hammer-ons and ghost notes. Pluck the lower note with your first finger, so that the longer second finger is ready and waiting to play the octave.

Preparing finger placement ahead of time is crucial, especially when playing fast, syncopated lines like this. Have a "one finger in the future" mentality when working on your technique.

One thing to notice about this line is how effective using very simple notes can be!

Example 5e

Les Claypool

The techniques of Les Claypool could take up an entire book. We've got just five examples, so let's start with his highly rhythmic slapping, which he bases on the style of three greats – Larry Graham, Louis Johnson and Stanley Clarke.

Use the bony part of your thumb to strike the strings roughly where the fretboard ends, keeping it parallel to the E string. Bounce off the string immediately, so it vibrates fully.

Keep your fretting hand thumb behind the neck and pat all your fingers (which should be flat) across all the strings. All the ghost notes are muted using this patting technique.

Use your third and fourth fingers for the E and F notes on frets 7 and 8, and keep your fretting hand in one position the entire line.

The last three notes are 1/16th note triplets – three notes in the space of half a beat. Pop the first note with your first finger then hammer down onto the remaining notes.

Listen to the audio example to catch the rhythm.

Example 5f

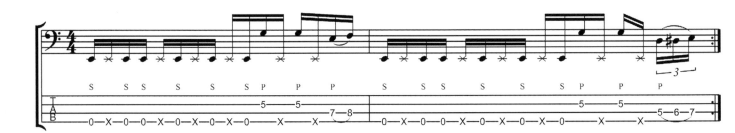

Using hammer-ons, slides and pull-offs in conjunction with the thumb and first finger yields impressive results. This is a complicated riff, so we'll need to break it down.

"L.H. Pat" stands for "left hand pat". Flatten out your fingers and slap them against muted strings as you did in Example 5f.

The ghost notes are slapped with the thumb.

Combining these techniques distributes ghost notes between both hands, which allows intricate rhythmic figures to be played.

Slide from fret 5 to 4 using your first finger before playing the D on fret 5 with your second finger and hammering on with your fourth finger. Then return back into position with your first finger hovering over fret 5. You can make that shift while playing the open E string.

For the strummed chord at the end of the riff use your fingernails, or thumb and first finger held together, as though holding a plectrum. If you use your fingernails, flick your fingers out, down towards the floor like a flamenco guitarist. Claypool uses root and 5th power chords like this a lot. Fret it with fingers 1 and 3 or 1 and 4, whichever you find easiest.

Example 5g

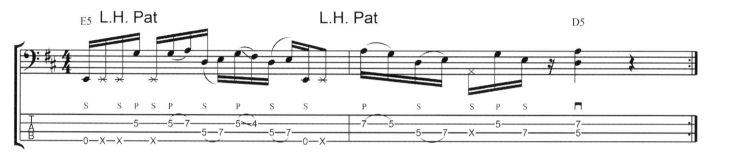

Mood and *colour* are very important in rock music and can be created via many musical devices, but one of the most important is the choice of key/scale. Here's the exact same riff as before, this time using E Phrygian.

We've encountered this mode before. The b2 in the scale gives it a dark rock sound. In this key, that's the movement from E to F. Here's a useful shape for you to experiment with this sound.

E Phrygian

Example 5h can be played in an almost identical way to the previous example, but more of a shift is needed to strum the power chord. Make that shift during the rest, being as quick as you can after you've slapped the E.

Example 5h

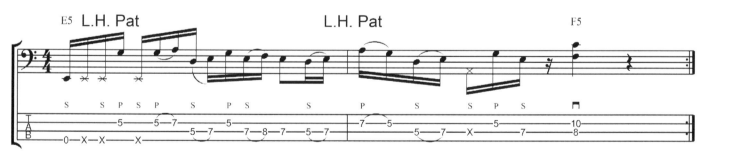

A common theme to Claypool riffs is driving, insistent 1/4 note riffs such as this next one. He uses all kinds of slapping and strumming techniques but the next example uses just strumming. Use either the flamenco fingernails technique described in the previous example or the imaginary-plectrum-in-fingers approach.

Either way, keep a constant down-up motion going with the picking hand. This is how guitarists approach rhythm playing and is a way of locking into the groove and keeping the up and down strokes consistent. Follow the markings closely and listen to the audio example to familiarise yourself with the underlying triplet feel.

The symbols in bars two and three (%) mean to repeat the bar before. Be prepared for the hand shifts back and forth between the hammer-on line and the E power chords. Keep those power chords short in length and aim to get the whole riff up to 125bpm.

Example 5i

Let's take a look at another strummed riff. If you need to, you can anchor your thumb on the E string or top of the fretboard to give the strumming hand more stability.

This time we'll use power chords with an added octave to fill out the sound more (compare the diagrams below).

You can play the octave power chord either with fingers 1, 3 and 4, or by barring the third or fourth finger on the 5th and octave notes.

E Power Chord (Root & 5th)

E Power Chord (Root 5th & octave)

The power chord shapes are mixed up in this example. As you make the shifts, maintain the power chord shape with your hand.

Example 5j

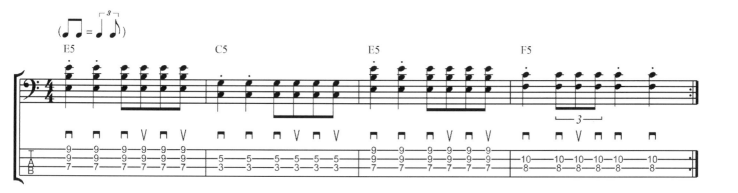

Doug Wimbish

We kick off the Wimbish-style examples with a Dorian riff at 95bpm. Concentrate in particular on the timing of the hammer-ons in this one. If you want, you can use the fourth finger for all the notes on the 3rd fret, or the third finger if you find that easier.

Example 5k

A bit like Les Claypool, Wimbish has the full array of bass techniques under his fingers and likes to use more than one within a riff. The next example is a fast line that switches from fingerstyle to slap then back again.

Slide up to the 10th fret from below before sliding back down to the Bb on fret 1. During the Bb at the end of bar three, there is enough time to alter your hand position from fingerstyle to slap. Isolate the last bar and go through the slap markings carefully, building up speed and making sure you bounce the thumb off the string while getting the first finger under the D string, ready for the pops.

Example 5l

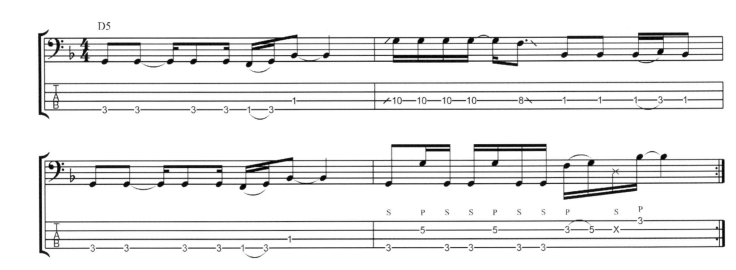

Similarly, work slowly through the slap markings for the next example. The line is a repetitive, almost tribal-sounding rhythm that should be played at 100bpm. Make sure the hammer-ons sound as loud as the slapped notes and pay attention to the coordination between the hands.

Once you get this together, aim to hit the bass like a drummer would strike the drum skins. The key to excellent slap timing is to get that drum-like consistency going, counting in 1/16ths in this case.

Example 5m

There's a backing track to practice the rhythms in the next example. The tempo is a steady 85bpm and there are 1/16th note triplets as well as swung 1/16ths. The best way to hear how to play these rhythms is to listen to the audio example. Swung 1/16ths at this tempo sound really funky and it's a feel you should know how to play.

Pluck the first two 1/6th note triplets with alternating fingers then *rake* the finger playing the second note onto the D string. i.e. after plucking the G string, allow the finger to travel *through* the string to make contact with the D string, without lifting it up.

That will be first, second, second, or second, first, first, depending on which finger you started plucking with. Raking is a great technique to generate speed.

Then, you need a quick hand shift to get to the 1st fret. You can make that shift as you're playing the ghost note, right after the C on the 3rd fret.

Example 5n

The previous riff was in C minor. When you're playing any bassline and you want to add in a fill, knowing this information is essential as it tells you what scale notes to use.

Let's take the same line and add a fill at the end of bar four. The fill uses notes from the C Minor Blues scale (a minor pentatonic scale with an added b5). Minor blues scales are perfect for minor keys.

Learn this shape and use the backing track to create your own fills in the same place as the example. The b5 is highlighted as a hollow circle. That interval is used in *so* many minor rock basslines, so learn it well!

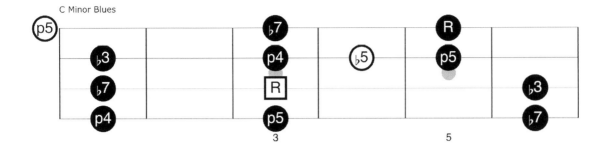

In the next example, after the pull-off in the last bar, quickly shift to fret 1 as you play the ghost note. It really doesn't matter exactly where you play the ghost note as long as you get that dead, percussive sound. Using ghost notes and open strings (where possible) to shift makes intricate lines like this one much easier to play.

Example 5o

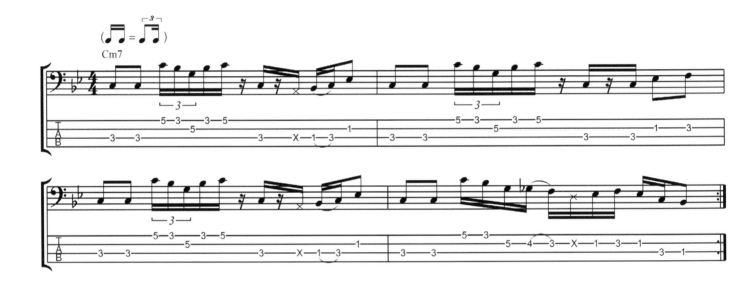

If you want to explore funk bass a little more, check out my book *100 Funk Grooves For Electric Bass*.

Chapter 6: Grunge

Not many cities can lay claim to being the epicentre of a musical movement, but just as Detroit spawned Motown, so Seattle gave birth to grunge.

This alternate rock style sprang up in the West Coast port city and surrounding areas, fusing together metal and punk sub genres. The lyrics were angst fuelled and the music often angry, aggressive and devoid of the technical prowess of other rock styles.

Nirvana's *Nevermind* album helped make grunge the most popular genre of rock from the early to mid-90s. Krist Novoselic, a founder member of Nirvana, was heavily influenced by the classic rock bands of the '60s and '70s. His playing style is simple when it needs to be and intricate at other times.

Novoselic's tone is bright, focused and direct, generated by plectrum downstrokes and fresh stainless-steel strings. He fills out the trio format with busy, intricate lines with his thick, Gibson Thunderbird bass tone.

Formed in 1990, Pearl Jam were the decade's other monster grunge act. Bassist Jeff Ament was one of the founder members and the band quickly found huge success with their album *Ten*. Not only did Ament take care of bass duties, he was one of the main songwriters too. This top-down approach can be heard in his playing style, which is very much for the song.

Obsessed with the tone and feel the bass brings to a song, Ament was known for embracing different textures in the form of upright, fretless, and all kinds of different bass guitars.

Mike Starr died tragically young of a drug overdose in 2011. It was his addiction to drugs that led him to leave Alice In Chains at the height of their powers in 1993. Ably replaced by Mike Inez, Starr remains something of a fan favourite. He played melodically, favouring a plectrum and an overdriven tone, although he did play with fingers occasionally.

Gear checklist: Novoselic is most famous for playing a Gibson Thunderbird bass with Rotosound stainless steel strings. He has played many other basses though, including a Gibson Ripper and Ibanez Black Eagle. In the Nirvana era he used an Ampeg 400T and a ProCo Rat pedal.

Jeff Ament is one of those players who uses a lot of different basses. He has often used a Wal fretless and Modulus, as well as various Fender Precisions, electric uprights, acoustic basses and a Hamer 12-string. Some people are one brand players, but Jeff definitely is not. He did, however, team up with Mike Lull to make a series of basses. He has mainly used Ampeg amplification.

Mike Starr played mainly Spector basses (with PJ pickup configuration) and Ampeg amps and cabs.

Recommended Listening:

Lounge Act – Nirvana

Stay Away – Nirvana

In Bloom – Nirvana

Them Bones – Alice In Chains

We Die Young – Alice In Chains

Would? – Alice In Chains

Even Flow – Pearl Jam

Oceans – Pearl Jam

Animal – Pearl Jam

Krist Novoselic

Nirvana riffs are often quite angular with no real attention paid to the key centre. This results in angsty sounding riffs like this example. Play the 1/8ths quite fast, somewhere around 130bpm, and pick with downstrokes throughout. Alternatively, use your fingers but really dig in, to coax out as much aggression as possible.

Example 6a

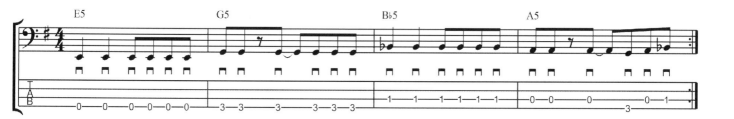

Play the next riff along with the previous one as it's equally odd but somehow works! Picked (or plucked) 1/8th notes are the heartbeat of rock bass playing. It's one of the most common rhythms in the genre and not one to turn your nose up at (even though they look and seem easy).

Aim to keep the notes the same length with no deviation in tempo, tone or volume – it's not as easy as it appears. Set your metronome to 130bpm and meditate on this groove till you lock it in.

Example 6b

There's a backing track for this next example – a furious punk riff to be played with downstrokes. A riff like this takes stamina to play, so use the backing track to build up yours. If at any point you feel any strain, particularly in the picking hand wrist, stop playing. This riff sounds great with some distortion.

Example 6c

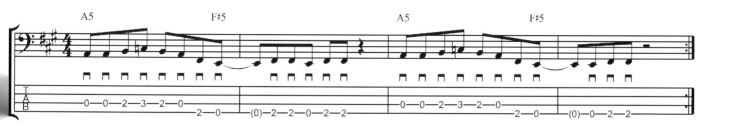

One of the best Nirvana moments ever is the opening to *Lounge Act* with its twisted harmony and zingy, bright bass riff. Example 6d emulates that style and starts with an A minor triad before ending with a characteristic Novoselic slide.

This is another fast one (around 170bpm), so if downstrokes fly by too quickly, play the 1/8ths with alternate picking. The slide in the last bar is a shift slide, so make sure to pick (or pluck) the Bb on the 6th fret.

Example 6d

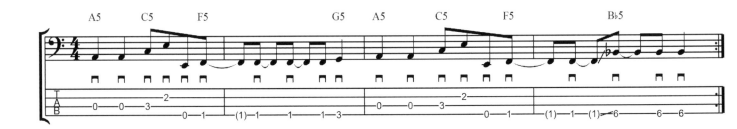

This next riff can be played using all alternate picking. It all happens on the E string, so there's no need to move the picking hand, which should be anchored to provide stability. Rest the heel of your hand on the body above the E string to achieve greater accuracy when picking.

Make sure the down and up strokes are consistent, with only the tip of the plectrum coming into contact with the string, and that you're not picking too far either side of the string. This will ensure that your plectrum technique is secure and your tone is even. Try using just downstrokes, then return to alternate picking, aiming to make the notes sound the same as with downstrokes.

Use the backing track to practice these techniques.

Example 6e

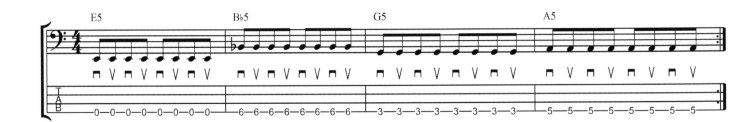

Jeff Ament

Ament can play aggressively, but also likes to access the softer side of bass playing, fitting into any song. He loves using harmonics with a fretless bass, but they sound equally good on fretted basses.

Pluck the harmonics with first and second fingers while fretting both notes with your fourth finger.

Example 6f

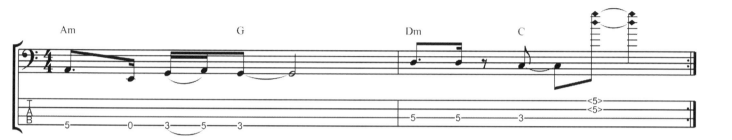

You can hear a Paul McCartney influence in some of Ament's more melodic bass hooks. The next example sits on an A Minor Pentatonic groove. Make up some of your own fills at the end of the phrase by using the G, A, D and E notes on frets 3 and 5 of the E and D string. You can stay in that one place for the entire riff.

Example 6g

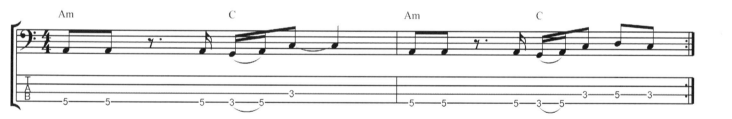

The next riff is a modified version of the previous one, heading up the neck to create a high register hook. Have your thumb positioned roughly behind the 9th fret, then pivot on it, sliding to the 14th fret with your third finger. Keep your thumb behind that 9th fret and shift back to your first finger on the 10th fret C note. Then slide back down on the repeat.

Articulations like slides add interest to an otherwise potentially bland bassline. Do experiment with the exact positioning of your thumb pivot behind the neck.

Example 6h

Jeff Ament is a master of crafting memorable basslines using simple notes and rhythms. The next example follows suit by using a repetitive rhythm with root notes and *inversions*.

When you invert a chord, you play a note other than the root in the bass (as explained earlier in Chapter Three). Inversions allow us to compose more creative basslines. Instead of playing root notes all the time, the bassist can choose to play other notes in the arpeggio, which often means smoother transitions between chords, and lines that are more melodic.

Inversions are written as *slash chords*. The letter on the left is the chord name and the letter on the right is the bass note to be played. In bar three, C/E is a first inversion C major chord, with the 3rd (E) in the bass.

Example 6i

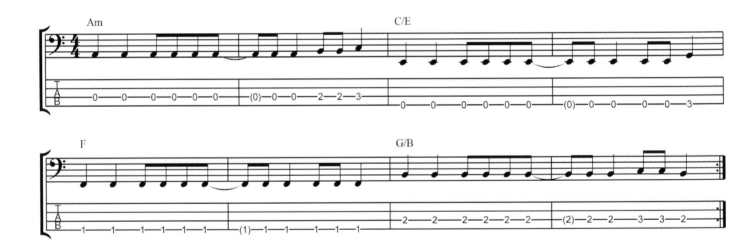

This fast riff uses the open A string to keep the riff on two strings. This makes it easier to play and avoids any unnecessary string crossing. Control the open A by gently touching the string with your fretting hand fingers. If the rhythm is too fast, slow the tempo and gradually build up to full speed.

Example 6j

Mike Starr

You can play this first Mike Starr-style riff entirely in 3rd position, stretching out to the Eb on fret 6 with your fourth finger. Starr's scratchy tone comes from his Spector bass and use of a plectrum. It's a good skill to be able to play any riff with a pick or fingers, so try both ways.

Example 6k

If you listen to *Would?* you'll hear that scratchy signature Mike Starr tone. To get the tone, angle your plectrum as you strike the strings so that you drag it across the windings of the string.

Use alternate picking and closely follow the plectrum markings, anchoring your picking hand so that your picking becomes more consistent. Play this riff at 95bpm.

Example 6l

Alice In Chains had a punk energy but were also influenced by classic rock riffs, like this next example. Keep your foot tapping on the beats, focusing on the off beats (where your foot comes up off the floor). When you count like this it's easier to subdivide the beats and tighten up your timing.

Example 6m

The next riff uses an interesting mode known as the Mixolydian b6, which has a spacey, psychedelic vibe to it. This is the fifth mode of the Melodic Minor scale and was used by Led Zeppelin in some of their more experimental songs (such as *Ten Years Gone*).

Here is a one octave E Mixolydian b6 scale (mode five of A Melodic Minor). It is almost identical to the regular E Mixolydian scale, apart from having a b6, hence its name.

Experiment with it to construct some spacey-sounding riffs!

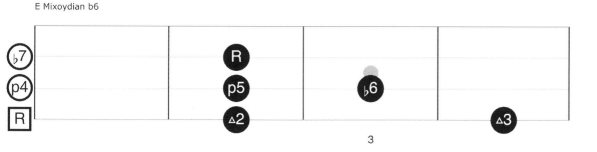

Example 6n

Example 6o uses the same rhythms and tempo but converts the riff into a more traditional sounding E Minor Blues scale. Compare the mood of the Mixolydian b6 riff of the previous example to this more "meat and potatoes" sound.

The following is a useful shape to use when composing your own riffs.

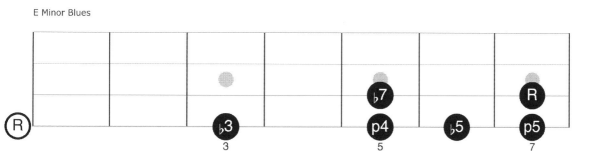

Example 60

Chapter 7: Modern Rock

Modern rock is a term describing rock music from around the mid-to-late 1970s onwards. It tends to lean more towards alternative rock acts but is broad enough for me to include three diverse but great bass players! Bands from this genre of rock feature prominently on radio stations around the world, due to their commercial nature.

Faith No More are a band that is hard to categorise due to the diverse nature of their influences. They rap, play hard metal riffs, and have covered Burt Bacharach (*This Guy's In Love With You*). All these disparate styles come together to form one of the greatest alternative rock bands ever.

Their bass player, Billy Gould, is one of the most underrated players. He has a monstrous rock tone and a unique hard attack that makes his playing unmistakable. Not surprisingly, given the myriad influences going on, Gould uses slap, plectrum or fingerstyle depending on the song.

Listen to *Everything's Ruined* for a creative slap line, *Superhero* for some face melting plectrum work, and *Evidence* for smooth, soulful fingerstyle technique. Bass players on forums regularly lock horns over the plectrum versus fingers debate, but listening to these three songs should be enough to convince anyone of the merits of learning all three.

Chris Wolstenholme from Muse has perhaps the most impressive effects board/rack of all time. Doug Wimbish may take umbrage with that statement, but Wolstenholme's use of effects is legendary. His setup is so complex that he gets his bass tech to switch sounds on and off from the side of the stage.

Primarily a fingerstyle player, he sometimes switches to plectrum, such as on *Assassin*. Muse can be intense and their style of music requires prodigious stamina and technique. Tone is central to Wolstenholme's bass style but it's his technique and musical creativity that set him apart as one of rock bass's finest.

Muse are commercially successful but talented enough to influence prog bands like Dream Theater (check out the *Octavarium* album).

One of the most innovative and remarkable rock bass players of the last twenty years is Mike Kerr from Royal Blood. The band consists of only drums and bass, and Kerr gets his instrument to sound like a bass and a guitar at the same time. He uses a plethora of amps, effects and switching systems to pull this off.

Kerr himself says that he's not that knowledgeable when it comes to bass (or guitar) technique. When he learned hammer-ons he wrote one of the band's biggest hits *Figure It Out*. Despite being self-taught, Kerr relies on his ear and his unique hybrid bass/guitar tones to come up with some incredible riffs. These riffs often rely on space and rhythm to fill the sonic spectrum – both of which powerful forces in Royal Blood songs. Kerr talks about the importance of removing notes from riffs until you have something where the gaps are as important as the notes.

Gear checklist: Billy Gould is a long time Zon Sonus user and has a signature model with a built-in fuzz circuit. He used a Gibson Grabber for the first two records before being endorsed by Aria and playing the Aria Pro II SB-Integra. Central to his tone is the use of fresh, out of the box strings, lately Dunlop Nickels. He uses Peavey amps and cabs.

There's no real standard Muse bass sound as Wolstenholme changes things up all the time. He uses Status bass guitars and has his own signature model, although he also plays various Fenders, Gibsons and Rickenbackers. Detailing his complex setup would require a chapter of its own, but his favourite pedals include the Electro-

Harmonix Big Muff, Human Gear Animato and Akai Deep Impact. He uses three Marshall DBS 700 amps going into Mills bass cabs with various different settings that his tech switches between.

Mike Kerr is another bass player with a complex setup necessitated by his need to be a guitarist and bass player at the same time! He's more comfortable on short scale basses and currently plays a 30" scale length Fender Jaguar. Pedals include an Electro-Harmonix POG2, Boss Harmonist and Tech 21 Red Ripper.

Recommended Listening:

Everything's Ruined – Faith No More

Stay Away – Faith No More

Superhero – Faith No More

Supermassive Black Hole – Muse

Panic Station – Muse

Hysteria – Muse

Figure It Out – Royal Blood

Boilermaker – Royal Blood

Oblivion – Royal Blood

Billy Gould

This first Gould-style example is a 160bpm picked riff that requires a lot of stamina. Use downstrokes throughout, except for the 1/16th notes where you introduce an upstroke. Otherwise, keep a steady 1/8th note bounce going with your wrist. There's a little jump to watch out for from the E on the 7th fret to the low G.

Example 7a

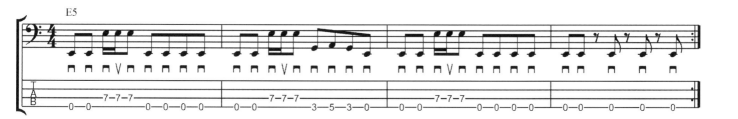

The b2 is a metal-sounding interval we've already come across but there's another useful interval that's cut from the same cloth. In the following example, the root is E and Bb is the b5. It's very dark sounding in a rock context and you can also hear the b2 (F) at play in this riff.

Example 7b

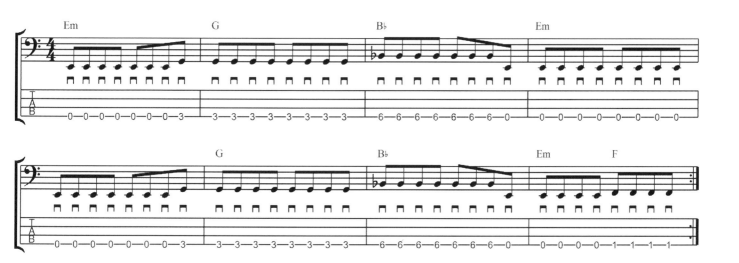

You can combine Example 7c with the previous riff. It's up to you whether you use downstrokes, alternate picking or fingers. The upside of using all downstrokes is a more consistent, driving feel (which you should continue to aim for if using alternate picking).

Example 7c

Faith No More's drummer, Mike Bordin, is renowned for his tribal drum beats that make use of the tom toms. Gould will often simply follow the pattern in his basslines, emphasising the rhythms more than the notes. The key here is to break the line down into one "unit" of two beats and get that sounding tight. The rest of the line repeats.

Example 7d

Gould's playing is sometimes quirky, with articulations and unconventional note choices contributing to unusual riffs. A great example is the verse on *Everything's Ruined*.

The next example uses slides, vibrato and short notes in a fingerstyle line. Pluck the first note then slide one fret higher and back in one movement. Use your third or fourth finger for that, so you can reach for the C note with your first finger.

Most of the time, subtle vibrato is what you want on bass but here, throw taste out of the window! Really bend the string up and down quickly to get some metal vibrato, then jump to fret 15 before sliding back down to the 5th fret.

Example 7e

Chris Wolstenholme

One of the most iconic basslines of all time is *Hysteria* with its machine gun 1/16th notes and open string pedals. The next example is in a similar style, played at 100bpm.

There's a backing track to play along to but you might need to take this one slowly before you attempt it at full speed. Once you have it down, it's a case of fluidly shifting your hand from high up to low down on the neck and back. This line calls for good coordination, dexterity and stamina, all of which you will build as you practice it.

Example 7f

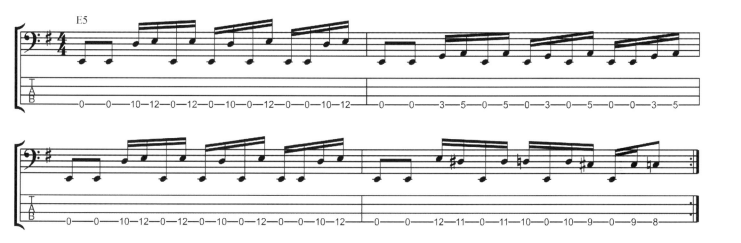

The *Hysteria* bassline uses open strings to jump around so let's take the previous riff and head over to the A string in the last bar.

Example 7g

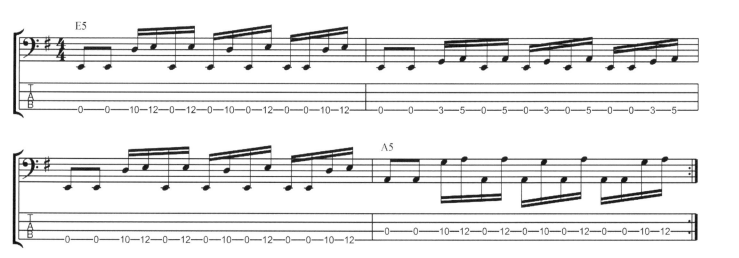

The next riff is a hat tip to classic rock. It's a 4/4 shuffle which is a fun meter to play. Count four beats per bar and subdivide each beat into triplets. Stomp on your favourite distortion and/or synth pedal and rock out!

Example 7h

Lead singer and guitarist Matt Bellamy is the chief Muse songwriter and is hugely influenced by classical music. Classical composers were well known for their use of arpeggios and inversions. It's often the case that a cool bassline can be written by simply following the outline of the chord tones while playing a repeating rhythmic phrase. That's the idea behind Example 7i.

Most of the notes are chord tones with the occasional note from the key of E Minor using the E Natural Minor scale to add some melody.

Example 7i

Example 7j follows suit with a relentless 1/16th note (85bpm) groove built around the following minor 7th arpeggio shape. There are literally hundreds of basslines that have been built using these simple notes, so learn them well (*Livin' On A Prayer* and *Billie Jean* are two that spring to mind).

Minor 7th arpeggio - R 5 b7 octave

To play this accurately requires good technique and stamina. Follow the suggested fingering pattern then shift quickly to the other positions using the same shape and fingering. To get the changes bang in time, focus on jumping to the root note of the chord with your first finger. The rest should follow.

Example 7j

Mike Kerr

It's important to keep the note lengths short on this Kerr-style riff, otherwise it won't sound right. Use the open E string notes to shift down to the 3rd fret and make sure to anticipate the C# on fret 4. That note falls on the last 1/16th of beat four.

It's a good idea to subdivide the beat into 1/16ths and count "4 e & **a**" for that note in order to nail its placement.

Example 7k

There's a backing track for the next riff. Once again, keep the note lengths short and really dig in to inject as much attitude as you can. This is a fairly simple riff but it's all about how you attack the strings and how you make it feel. The space is as important as the notes you play.

Example 7l

The next one's a fun one, taking a leaf out of Kerr's book to play like a bass player *and* guitarist at the same time. The low notes are the bass part and the high notes the fancy guitar response.

This riff uses the G Minor Pentatonic scale – one of the most common rock scales. Use the shape below to make up your own bass "call" and guitar "response" lines similar to Example 7m.

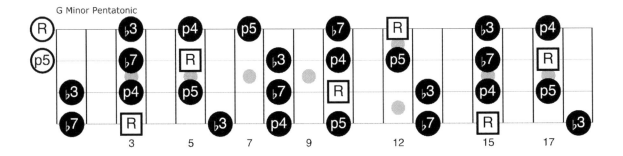

Example 7m

Rock riffs can appear very simple on the surface but if you don't pay attention to note length, attack, tone and feel, a riff can fall flat on its face. Intent is a hard thing to explain let alone teach but if there's one thing you can take away from rock bass playing it's that *how* you play something will define the emotional impact on the listener.

Take the next bassline. Listen to the audio example to hear how you can alter the length of 1/8th notes, playing some a bit longer than others, and how this livens up the notes.

Example 7n

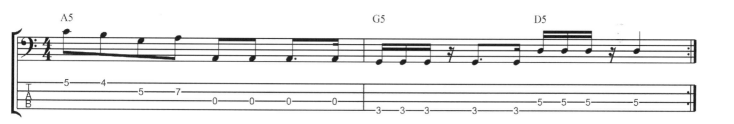

Above all, Mike Kerr is a master of space. The last example gives the drums plenty of room to shine by using lots of rests.

Lock in with the drums and guitar on the backing track. Take the notes in this riff (G, A, C and D) and make up similar riffs by changing the order of the notes and altering the rhythms. Keep the repeating pattern with lots of space idea going and you will come up with loads of cool lines!

Example 7o

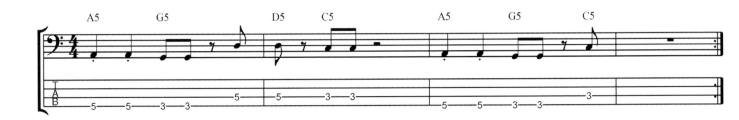

Essential Listening

Here's a reminder of the Spotify playlist that contains all the recommended listening from this book. Simply scan the code with your smartphone.

I highly recommend digging into a particular player's style by listening to one of their albums all the way through. With the ability to stream anything, anytime, this is actually a tough discipline these days, but it's worth doing! Deeper listening not only sparks inspiration and ideas but is also immensely pleasurable.

Make part of your practice routine a regular listening session where you choose an album and listen to it from start to finish.

Albums *used* to be written with all the songs forming a coherent thread from start to finish. You should listen to anything and everything, but here are ten classics:

1. *The Dark Side of the Moon* – Pink Floyd

2. *Rumours* – Fleetwood Mac

3. *London Calling* – The Clash

4. *Nevermind* – Nirvana

5. *Metallica* – Metallica

6. *Ok Computer* – Radiohead

7. *Led Zepellin II* – Led Zeppelin

8. *A Night at the Opera* – Queen

9. *Electric Ladyland* – The Jimi Hendrix Experience

10. *Moving Pictures* – Rush

Rock Bass Gear

The modern-day bassist has never had it so good when it comes to gear. There's a bewildering range of equipment involving all manner of things like amp modelling, analogue/digital effects, multi effects and more.

The choice is fantastic but it's *way* too easy to get lost in the details. It's also the case that G.A.S. (Gear Acquisition Syndrome) is a real thing to be (mostly) avoided!

In this section I'll give you some gear tips that will set you on the right path to tone nirvana, while hopefully proving to be wallet friendly.

What bass and strings?

Rock bass players tend to go for bright, aggressive tones that can cut through a mix.

That's why you rarely come across the use of flatwound strings which sound mellower than the zingy stainless strings most players favour. Go for the latter.

If you need to go below E, consider a 5-string. If you prefer 4-strings, one option is to install a Hipshot Detuner, which can drop the E down to a D and even lower at the flick of a lever.

You can also experiment with tuning your bass down, but make sure you have a neck that can take this. Use higher gauge strings so that the tension is maintained.

On the subject of strings, lighter gauges (like 40-60-80-100) are easier to play, which might be useful if you're playing fast passages. On the flip side, you might get a slightly thinner tone so 45-55-65-105 is a good starting point.

I own a Lakland fretless bass that Pino Palladino used in the '80s and a 1968 Fender Precision. Both are worth over £3000 but my best rock bass is a 1982 Ibanez Roadster purchased for around £350. It wasn't a model on my radar but I played it in a shop and instantly loved it.

I highly recommend you get yourself down to your nearest bass shop and try a few basses out. Look for a resonant, bright rock bass tone. Go in with an open mind and you may surprise yourself.

Good rock bass brands include Fender (Jazz and Precision), Ibanez, Spector and MusicMan. All of them offer budget-friendly options.

Amplifiers

Many amps (such as Ashdown and Ampeg models) have tubes that can be pushed into an overdriven signal. These are great, but tend to be heavy and expensive, so the alternative is a solid state or digital amp.

Sure, nothing can beat a big powerful tube amp with an 8x10 speaker cabinet. Nothing, that is, apart from a healthy back! These days, you can get a great rock tone from amp modellers and/or effects.

Effects

Sound processing plays an important role in rock bass tone. Start with a good bass and fresh strings on a well setup instrument. From there, the main rock effects are:

- Overdrive – for subtle harmonic saturation through to a high gain tone

- Distortions and fuzz – a more aggressive square-wave signal that is commonly heard in rock

- Compression – a compressor evens out your tone, taming the peaks and bringing up the lows. Tony Levin uses compression like an effect occasionally to sustain long notes

- EQ – an equaliser turns up or cuts the volume of specific frequencies in the audio spectrum. It's a fantastic device that you can use to shape your tone

Boutique brands like Strymon and Wren and Cuff make expensive pedals but Boss and Mooer produce cheap pedals that sound great.

Just remember that you need to supply the low end in a band and pedals will often rob you of that. Ideally, buy pedals that have a blend control or ones known to preserve the low frequencies. One example is the Malekko Diabolik – a modern-day classic bass fuzz designed to keep your lows intact.

Next Steps

Rock bass is about aggression, attitude and creativity. The best way to learn about those things is by listening to a broad range of rock styles.

Alongside learning the riffs in this book, think about your tone. Tone, timing and technique are the essential three "Ts". If you find yourself struggling, for example, with hammer-ons, then make the decision to master those in your next practice sessions.

Technique is your means of expression, so you need to have a wide range securely locked into your muscle memory. Play those techniques in time with fantastic tone and you're good to go.

Use a practice journal and identify the areas where you need to improve. This sort of self-analysis will ensure that you're always getting a tiny bit better. Over time, those small margins will compound and you *will* become a great bassist.

I'm always here to help you. If you'd like to reach out to me any time, you can do so via the links below. I also have hundreds of free lessons over on my YouTube channel, including plenty on how to create rock riffs and craft rock bass tones. See you there.

Above all, keep playing every day and keep refining your craft.

Good luck!

Dan

Connect with Dan

Instagram: **OnlineBassCourses**

YouTube: **OnlineBassCourses**

www.onlinebasscourses.com

If you got something from this book, I'd be eternally grateful if you would leave an Amazon review. It helps independent authors a huge amount if you do, and it allows people like me to write more books to help you on your bass playing journey.

Made in United States
Troutdale, OR
11/24/2024

25256158R00051